THE BAPT
AN

Merry Christmas 1996.
To KELVIAN + NELSON.

With lots of love
from
Mummy
Obot.

New Dawn books by Hugh Black

The
Baptism in the Spirit and Its Effects

Hugh B. Black

NEW DAWN BOOKS
GREENOCK, SCOTLAND

ISBN 1 870944 00 3

Unless otherwise stated, biblical references
are to the Revised Version.

Production and Printing in England for
NEW DAWN BOOKS
10A Jamaica Street, Greenock, Renfrewshire, PA15 1YB by
Nuprint Ltd, Station Road, Harpenden, Herts AL5 4SE.

Dedication

*To the memory of Charles G. Finney and J. Hudson Taylor,
whose lives and teachings have profoundly affected me.*

Acknowledgements

My thanks are due to:

The late Elizabeth H. Taylor and Robert M. Cleary for encouraging me to write.

My wife Isobel, daughters Alison and Mary, Pauline Anderson, Jennifer Jack and Irene Morrison for script reading, wise counsel and technical support.

Allan Wiggins and James and Maureen Lunan for supplying the material at short notice for Part 2 of the revised edition.

Contents

Preface to the Second Edition

In 1987 we published *Reflections on the Baptism in the Holy Spirit* and are now faced with the need for a reprint. We have taken the opportunity to change the title and add substantial material.

Thus Part 1 of the present book is a resetting of the earlier work with the addition of minor amendments. It is also supported by a brief but very important appendix with evidence that Charles G. Finney, Dwight L. Moody and Charles H. Spurgeon all spoke in tongues. Part 2 contains two unusual testimonies which show very clearly some of the *effects* of the baptism in the Spirit. Their inclusion provides a very appropriate balance to the teaching contained in Part 1.

Preface to the First Edition

Over recent decades there have been few issues which have more deeply exercised the church of Christ than the doctrine of the baptism in the Holy Spirit. Indeed the very term is controversial since the phrase is not used in precisely that way in the New Testament although the verb 'baptize' is so used. Feelings have often run very deep, as long-held traditional beliefs have been challenged.

There still exists a wide range of opinion about what, for example, is involved in the baptism; when it occurs— whether at salvation or as a later and separate experience; whether it is necessarily accompanied by 'tongues'. This present work attempts not only to interpret Scripture faithfully but to link the subject to present-day experience. The writer has been 'pentecostal' for over forty years and has been present when literally thousands have come into the fulness of the experience. The work is presented in the hope that it will help to heal breaches in the Body of Christ and bring illumination to some who may be in sincere confusion.

Part One

The Baptism in the
Holy Spirit

1

The Recent Background

In most evangelical circles, in the earlier part of this century, it was taught that the Holy Spirit was received at conversion and, in so far as any consideration was given to statements such as that of John the Baptist: 'He shall baptize you with the Holy Ghost and with fire', it was assumed that this took place at the time of the new birth. Groups of people, however, in many parts of the world including America, India and various European countries claimed that they had received a distinctive experience in the Holy Spirit similar to that of the early disciples on the day of Pentecost and that this was quite different from their conversion experience.

Initially many of those affected had no wish to separate themselves from their churches—but often their churches resented their views and had no wish to have them within their folds. This led to the formation of various new denominations—the best known of which in Britain were the Assemblies of God, Elim Foursquare Gospel Alliance, the Apostolic Church, the Apostolic Faith Church and various independent works. The movement in many cases may be viewed as springing from the Azusa Street revival in Los Angeles in 1906. It reached Sunderland in 1907 and spread gradually through Britain. Wide publicity was given to pentecostal doctrine in the early days by the very suc-

15

cessful campaigns of evangelists like Stephen and George Jeffreys, Smith Wigglesworth and others. Outstanding healings acted like a magnet to draw vast crowds.

By mid-century things had quietened down and while there was growth within pentecostal circles the mainline churches were little affected and often little interested — but again events in America were to have a profound influence in Britain. An Anglican clergyman, Dennis Bennett, had a remarkable 'pentecostal' experience, as did many of his people. Wide publicity was given to the matter and in a comparatively short time thousands of Anglicans and Catholics were involved in what has become known as the charismatic movement. In Britain people with no 'pentecostal' background but with a hunger for God were affected in almost every Christian denomination. Initially there was no desire to leave their groupings but rather to stay within and spread the knowledge of their new-found relationship with God and, on this occasion, most of the denominations were more willing to retain their members and give consideration to their views than had earlier been the case. This new movement began in the sixties, and unity was preserved within its ranks in the early stages. A time came, however, when some felt that they could better serve God outwith the older denominations and establish something which, in their view, more closely corresponded with the New Testament pattern. As a result various groups have now come into being with a strong emphasis on discipleship and house meetings.

Thus a position has arisen where there are pentecostal groups of various shades, and charismatic groups, some within older denominations and some outside them, but not joined to the older pentecostal groups. Views on doctrine generally, and on the baptism in the Holy Spirit specifically, are not always identical.

The position relative to the baptism could possibly be summed up as follows.

Conservative evangelicals consider that the Spirit is

received at conversion and that there is no special later experience of baptism in the Spirit.

Pentecostals generally believe that the Spirit is received (in one sense of the word) at conversion but that the baptism in the Spirit is a different and separate experience.

Charismatics generally believe that the Spirit is received at conversion and the fulness or baptism is an outflow from that experience. There is not normally the drawing of a sharp divide between the two, although there is an appreciation that the fulness often comes later than conversion.

It should perhaps also be noted that there are differences where 'tongues' are concerned. Some conservative evangelicals consider that they are not in evidence in our day. Probably the majority of pentecostals consider them an essential part of the experience of the baptism in the Spirit. The charismatics believe in them and often experience them, but do not believe that they always necessarily accompany the baptism.

So—what say the Scriptures?

2

The Prediction of John the Baptist

In the present writer's view the baptism in the Spirit involves an encounter with God and the keynote is wonderfully sounded by John the Baptist. The first word we read that John spoke was 'Repent'. His message was direct and awful. It led to the confession of sin and deep heart-searching in those baptized in water. The message was never light and hypocrites were turned away. The man and the message seem to have been one.

Now it was that man who said:

> I indeed baptize you with water unto repentance: but he that cometh after me is mightier than I, whose shoes I am not worthy to bear: he shall baptize you with the Holy Ghost and with fire: Whose fan is in his hand, and he will thoroughly cleanse his threshing-floor; and he will gather his wheat into the garner, but the chaff he will burn up with unquenchable fire (Mt 3:11–12).

We further read of John:

> On the morrow he seeth Jesus coming unto him and saith, Behold, the Lamb of God, which taketh away the sin of the world!...And John bare witness, saying, I have beheld the Spirit descending as a dove out of heaven; and it abode upon him. And I knew him not: but he that sent me to baptize with water, he said unto me, Upon whomsoever

thou shalt see the Spirit descending, and abiding upon him,
the same is he that baptizeth with the Holy Spirit (Jn 1:29,
32–3).

The sayings of John the Baptist deserve close scrutiny.
How Christians have rejoiced at the words, 'Behold the
Lamb of God that taketh away the sin of the world!' The
whole evangelical world says a glad 'Amen'. He was, and is,
the Lamb of God and He did indeed take away the sin of the
world in His atoning sacrifice. But mark—it was that same
John who said, 'He shall baptize you with the Holy Ghost
and with fire.' The same man said it about the same man. If
we accept the first how can we reject the second?

John also said, 'I indeed baptize you with water... but he
shall baptize you with the Holy Ghost and with fire.' Now
what kind of experience is John pointing to here? Might it
be reasonably paraphrased thus: I baptize with water, and
the flesh can be comparatively comfortable in water—but
He will baptize with fire, and the flesh cannot stand in fire?
He seemed to be indicating a profound and life-changing
experience—not something which would be so quiet and
casual as to go unnoticed but surely something phenomenal. For such an experience Crhistians should prepare
themselves very deeply.

This view is further strengthened by an examination of
the earlier quotation:

> Whose fan is in his hand, and he will thoroughly cleanse his
> threshing-floor; and he will gather his wheat into the garner,
> but the chaff he will burn up with unquenchable fire (Mt
> 3:12).

For some strange reason many seem to think of the burning
of the chaff and the gathering of the wheat into the barns as
related to a later day of judgment—but there is nothing in
the text to suggest this. Surely the truth is that with the
coming of the power of God the subject is profoundly
affected. Note the words: 'He will thoroughly purge his

threshing-floor'. There are purgings and purgings. I was brought up on a farm and was probably, as a result, dirtier than small boys normally are. I can still remember, after almost sixty years, my mother asking the ritual question: 'Have you washed your neck?' On receiving the ritual answer, 'Yes,' she conducted the ritual examination and usually said, 'You may have washed it, but now go and clean it.' My idea of washing did not meet her definition of cleaning. It usually ended with cold soapy water trickling down my rebellious neck after she took me by the ear to the kitchen sink. Note that when Christ cleanses, the cleansing is a real cleansing. The words are 'thoroughly purge'. If, from Christ's point of view, it is thorough, then thorough it will be. Surely in the hour of the baptism all chaff is burned up. The follies and false things go—only reality remains. The true things of the spirit endure. That which is real is gathered unto the Lord and preserved.

I have noticed over the years that, while many come seeking the baptism, not all are ready to receive. Some think that if they speak a few words in tongues all will be well. Some have no idea that an encounter with the divine is involved if there is to be true baptism. In many cases the first impact of God is to produce conviction—deep and awful conviction of sin—and sometimes the baptism does not take place at first seeking, and indeed not until sin has been dealt with. In true baptisms Matthew 3:12 is wonderfully fulfilled before our eyes.

It should be noted that, in addition to the Matthew and John scriptures previously quoted, Mark 1:8, Luke 3:16 and Acts 1:5 give us scriptural warrant for using the term baptism in the Spirit—for if one is baptized one receives a baptism and it is to the baptism that we refer.

The serious and vital place which Christ gives to the experience will be considered in its own context.

3

The Teaching of Christ
on the Holy Spirit

The gospels contain many references to the Holy Spirit. Christ Himself was born of Mary by the power of the Holy Spirit (Mt 1:18); Elizabeth and Zacharias, the parents of John the Baptist, were both filled with the Holy Spirit (Lk 1:41, 67); the Holy Ghost came upon Simeon, the aged prophet (Lk 2:25); Christ made it clear to Nicodemus that not only was the new birth essential for man, but this came by the action of the Spirit (Jn 3:5, 6, 8). He gave fearful warning of unpardonable sin—blasphemy against the Holy Spirit—when His enemies attributed to Beelzebub miracles which He wrought by the Spirit's power (Mt 12:31). He indicated that His followers should be baptized in water in the 'name of the Father and of the Son and of the Holy Ghost' (Mt 28:19).

In John 14:16–17, 26 and 16:7–15, Christ speaks of the Holy Spirit as the 'Comforter' and gives some indication of His work. He would teach the disciples; He would bring to their remembrance the sayings of Christ; the world He would convict of sin, righteousness and judgment; He would guide into all truth; He would declare things to come; He would glorify Christ.

There are, however, other references which are perhaps more pertinent to this particular enquiry.

In two of the gospels we read that after Christ was

baptized by John in the Jordan, the Holy Spirit came down upon Him in bodily form as a dove (Lk 3:22; Mt 3:16). We do not actually read that Christ was baptized in the Holy Spirit. Nor do we read that He had a 'holiness' or 'sanctification' experience. The fact is that Christ never was unholy or unsanctified. The Holy Spirit came down upon clean ground. For many years I was familiar with this part of Scripture but failed to see something of the depth of the truth it contained, and it was not until there came a linking with the words of Christ relative to blasphemy against the Holy Spirit, that particular illumination came, and so deep was the revelation that it could almost be described as life-changing. In the performance of His miracles Christ claimed that the Holy Spirit operated through Him. Suddenly I realized that for a lifetime there had been in me a deep subconscious assumption that Christ was different from us (which, of course, He is—but not always as we imagine it) and that He wrought His miracles on the ground of His deity. I suddenly realized that we never read this anywhere in Scripture. He wrought His miracles by the power of the Holy Spirit. In fact we read, 'But if I by the Spirit of God cast out devils, then is the kingdom of God come upon you' (Mt 12:28). The Spirit had come down upon Christ in a particular way on Jordan's banks. I went on to realize, and realize deeply, that if Christ, in the days of His flesh, became wholly dependent on the Holy Spirit, we dare not attempt to work the works of God in our own strength. This led me to seek deeply, not only to be filled with the Spirit but to endeavour to remain constantly under His control and to depend upon Him utterly in ministering. I became totally disillusioned with all human endeavour which was independent of Him. Nor was I satisfied with a measure of Him and me. It must be altogether Him.

I noted too that Christians were deeply divided so far as effective service for God was concerned. There was a very large group serving God zealously and honestly and often with comparatively little fruit. There were others—a much smaller group—who seemed to be far more God-dependent and whose fruit was rich and bountiful. Perhaps I could cite two cases.

Lessons from David Wilkerson

Some years ago there used to be regular Pentecostal Leaders' meetings in Scotland and frequently at these I taught the doctrine of complete dependence on the Holy Spirit. The doctrine was no doubt received with varying degrees of enthusiasm, but I never felt that all were wholly convinced. The day came when David Wilkerson came to Scotland and was powerfully used. I had always been an admirer of Mr Wilkerson and had particularly noted in *The Cross and the Switchblade* the hour when there was almost a gang riot when he gathered rival gangs in a public meeting. His singer had left the stage. The gangs were erupting. He came right to the end of his tether and cast himself wholly on God. Then the Holy Spirit came and the results were astounding. I found this perhaps the most interesting thing in the book. I have always been interested in hidden springs. I always want to know how spiritual things work. I found here a wonderful key—a key that the flesh is often too proud to use: total dependence on the Holy Spirit! I think David learned the lesson deeply. He certainly came to Glasgow depending on the Holy Spirit. I will never forget that visit. I think my order of three hundred tickets was the first received by the organizers—who gladly received it, fearing that a hall holding about four thousand might be half empty. The hall was filled and there stood a man obviously not a gifted human orator, but peculiarly clothed with the Holy Spirit, giving predictions about things to come and things which would happen that night. I was fascinated.

His predictions have been accurately fulfilled—the coming incidence of drug addiction in Glasgow and, perhaps more memorable, a prediction regarding the Beatles, who had not then broken up. John Lennon had some little time previously publicly and rather horribly blasphemed Christ. Mr Wilkerson said, 'Shortly the Beatles will not gather an audience anywhere in the world,' or words to that effect. They never did, although when it was said there was no indication of a rift. He went on to say, 'Tonight, before this meeting is over, young people will come down these aisles and the tears will be running down their cheeks.' I thought, 'David, you are in Scotland now, and for the first time. This doesn't happen in Scotland.' I had counselled at Billy Graham meetings and, while I saw many converted, I seldom saw a tear. He was right, however: they crowded down the aisles. The tears flowed powerfully. I was aware of the intense moving of the Holy Spirit, and this has had lasting results.

The next Pentecostal Leaders' meeting came along and Pastor John Phillips of Assemblies of God spoke to us about his experiences with David Wilkerson. He had arranged many of his meetings and travelled widely with him in Britain. I remember he said, 'You know, he was peculiarly God-led. It was strange working with him. When invitations to go on radio or TV came in, where others would have grasped at the opportunity, he was much more concerned to know what the Spirit was indicating to him.' In the life of David Wilkerson something of the relationship between dependence on the Holy Spirit and fruitfulness was wonderfully evident. I felt the doctrine I had so long taught was totally vindicated.

Can I reiterate the truth: if Christ Himself was wholly dependent on the Holy Spirit, how can we hope to work the works of God in our own strength?

And Kathryn Kuhlman

The second case I would cite is related to Kathryn Kuhlman. I had long been an admirer of this servant of God and was particularly interested in her healing ministry and in her teaching on healing. This is a subject which, in my view, has been very inadequately and often positively harmfully treated by many pentecostal writers and teachers. Blueprints are provided and they often do not work. People are blamed for having no faith, or for being in sin. Some teach that all should be healed and some believe that healing should be demanded. Frequently poor souls go empty away from healing services—not only with unhealed bodies but also with deeply upset souls.

Miss Kuhlman did not like some of the things she saw and sought God deeply on the subject, and some of the results of her ministry the Christian world generally knows. Her teaching on healing itself, however, is not so generally known. She maintained that she found no blueprint, no one formula. She noted that healing happened in different ways in Christ's own ministry. He could speak a word; He could make clay and put it on a man's eyes; the healing sometimes seemed to be dependent on a man's own faith, sometimes on the faith of another, or of others. The widow of Nain's son had no faith—nor had Lazarus! Kathryn found it exactly the same. It was essential to be dependent on the Holy Spirit, and He did things His way and He did things in a rich variety of ways. I discovered in her a writer (and a practitioner) who saw things exactly as I did. When this happens one is normally delighted and feels that at last a truly wise teacher has been found!

The day came when I had opportunity to hear Miss Kuhlman. My wife and I were on a visit to a daughter in Michigan some years ago and Miss Kuhlman was due to preach at Notre Dame University—within easy flying range. The meeting started at 2 p.m. and we were warned to be there by 10 a.m., because the hall only held about ten thousand and she had been there once before. The people were indeed queuing by 10 a.m. I remember it so clearly. I noted a nun with her group, and a number of men whom I took to be pastors. One—I think a wizened old Welshman—was explaining to the others that he did not generally agree with women ministry. 'God only used Deborah in Old Testament times because He could not find a man,' he declared. Similarly God was using Kathryn Kuhlman because He could not find a man in America! 'Well, well,' I thought, *'poor America!'* I was tempted, sorely tempted, to get into the fray—for I profoundly believe in women ministry—but on this occasion I held my peace. I get into quite enough trouble on my own side of the Atlantic without extending it to another continent.

And so we got inside, and in due time Kathryn came out and I was about to witness my first such American occasion. She came out full of life and animation and began to introduce her song-leader, her pianist and her choir, and they were all given 'big hands'—at that time an unheard of thing in Britain. Her choir leader she introduced as 'an Englishman who had been a Presbyterian from the crown of his head right down to the soles of his feet (including, I took it, a very rigid and unbending back) and then the Lord baptized him in the Holy Ghost! Give him a big hand.' There was nothing irreverent in it. There was a joy in it and I enjoyed it thoroughly. Then she got her eye on the nun whom I had noted in the queue. She was evidently a Mother Superior and Kathryn invited her on to the platform, which was remarkably like a boxing ring. Kathryn spoke a few kindly words to her and then laid hands on her, saying, 'I bless the Lord.' The nun measured her length backwards and lay there on the canvas for quite a time. Nobody appeared to be unduly concerned. It was evident that these things happened in Kathryn Kuhlman meetings.

Kathryn then began to speak and at the very outset made what I regarded as a very significant statement (paraphrased): 'I want to speak to you today about the Holy Spirit, but I must warn you that I may not be able to finish the sermon. I must obey the Spirit and if He comes in a particular way I will require to do exactly as I am told.' She did in fact finish the sermon and then the revelation ministry began—but not before I had a disappointing shock. She said, 'Now I am not going to lay hands on anybody for healing.' I really was disappointed, but then she added, 'God will heal you where you sit, and when you are healed you may come to the platform—but not before it.' As I said, there came the revelation ministry and this operated at tremendous speed. She indicated people all over the auditorium and told of their ailments and pronounced the will of God regarding their healings. All over the place people got to their feet and crowded down the aisles to the platform. Again and again she questioned individuals and laid on hands, blessing the Lord. Again and again they went down prostrate under His power. She called for doctors, any doctors in the building, to come forward and verify the things which were happening. Had I been a doctor I could have gone. One did where blindness had been healed. I remember the humour of the situation. After laying hands on the person healed, Kathryn laid hands on the doctor too and he, probably not a Christian, found himself going floorwards. She indicated that so strong was the power in the area where she was ministering that she could hardly stay on her own feet. Ushers obviously expected people to go down and stood behind. On one occasion not only was the person concerned affected but the person immediately behind and a third behind the second. Scores were healed and then suddenly she turned to salvation. Again they came in great numbers and were similarly dealt with.

What is the point of the story? She became dependent on the Holy Spirit and the whole world knows of the glory that came to God through a life that after very stormy days became so deeply God-possessed that vast numbers were richly blessed and the fruit was abundant. In the meeting described I saw the God-dependence outworked.

May I say it again: if Christ Himself wrought solely by the power of the Holy Spirit in His earthly ministry, dare we attempt to work the works of God in our own human strength?

As an ex-teacher I know the value of illustration—par-

ticularly interesting illustration—and all the world loves a
good story; so I make no apology for having gone down
these two side lines. There are many ways of teaching, and
sometimes if solid material is interspersed with illustration
it can be more easily understood and absorbed. I will
permit myself a third digression before getting back to hard
work.

A Forgotten Man

Many years ago I read of a man whose name I have long
forgotten. He was evidently very deeply used of God and
was once asked wherein lay the secret of his power and
fruitfulness. He was unwilling to comment but, on being
pressed, indicated that prior to a certain day in his life God
often spoke to him. Sometimes he obeyed; sometimes he
postponed obedience; sometimes he disobeyed. There
came, however, a day when he decided that if the great God
of Heaven deigned to speak to him, he would obey immediately. This he did, and he said that from that day blessing
flowed like a river. Surely it is the outworking of the principle of 'death to self'. As Paul said, 'I live; and yet no longer
I, but Christ liveth in me' (Gal 2:20).

Abiding in and Being Possessed by the Spirit

The second line of teaching which presents itself is related
to John 20:22: 'He breathed on them, and saith unto them,
Receive ye the Holy Ghost'. How often it is assumed that as
a result of this the Holy Spirit was immediately received—
but this was evidently not so, at least not in the sense of
receiving the baptism. He was later to charge them strictly
not to depart from Jerusalem until the enduement with
power came.

An extremely interesting and significant reference is contained in John 14:17–18. He spoke of 'the Spirit of truth:
whom the world cannot receive' and went on to say, 'ye

know him, for he abideth with you, and shall be in you.' Every individual who comes to Christ is born of the Spirit. There is no other way into the Kingdom. In such an hour a man is sealed with the Spirit and becomes a part of the body of Christ. At that moment he receives the Spirit: 'if any man hath not the Spirit of Christ, he is none of his,' Paul wrote (Rom 8:9). From that point he may expect to know the presence of the Spirit, to be guided, chided, comforted, led by the Spirit; he may grieve the Spirit; he may quench the Spirit. But none of this suggests that he has, by virtue of the new birth, or by receiving the Spirit, received the baptism of the Spirit. Surely Christ makes it plain: 'Ye know him...he abideth *with* you and shall be *in* you.' He drew a distinction between the *with* and the *in*. The Spirit was with them as an accompanying Power. He was in them in a general sense—but not in the possessing sense which was to come with the Acts 2 experience. Great controversy surrounds this point and it will be gone into more fully in a later context.

A Good Gift from our Heavenly Father

A third point we should note relates to an illustration used by Christ:

> And of which of you that is a father shall his son ask a loaf, and he give him a stone? or a fish, and he for a fish give him a serpent? Or if he shall ask an egg, will he give him a scorpion? If ye then, being evil, know how to give good gifts unto your children, how much more shall your heavenly Father give the Holy Spirit to them that ask Him? (Lk 11:11–13)

In this scripture men are envisaged as asking for the Holy Spirit—obviously as a distinct experience. Hence we have a right to do so and also to encourage others to ask specifically for this experience. It should not be assumed that it will happen automatically at conversion, or incidentally or by chance at some other time. It is viewed as a definite experience to be definitely sought and received.

In earlier days (although, to be fair, not so much now) some Christians objected: 'But how do I know what I will receive?' It is as though God anticipated this exact fear. How forcefully He puts it: 'Will a father give a son a stone for bread or a scorpion for a fish? And if you, who are evil, would not do such a thing, how can you ever imagine the heavenly Father not giving the Holy Spirit to those who ask Him?' (I paraphrase.) This should silence the critic fully and permanently.

Living Water

A fourth section relates to a promise of Christ:

> Now on the last day, the great day of the feast, Jesus stood and cried, saying, If any man thirst, let him come unto me, and drink. He that believeth on me, as the scripture hath said, out of his belly shall flow rivers of living water. But this spake he of the Spirit, which they that believed on him were to receive: for the Spirit was not yet given; because Jesus was not yet glorified (Jn 7:37–9).

Those who received the Holy Spirit in the baptismal sense were to find a perpetual outflow of life—like the spring of water promised to the woman at the well. In fact, with the baptism there is frequently this identical feeling. In my own case the sensation was exactly like a well pouring up constantly and gloriously. The up-welling is associated with the baptism.

Greater Works

Note also the reference to Christ's not yet being glorified. Christ was glad for their sakes that He was going away. Elsewhere He associated His departure with the coming of the Spirit and He also indicated that the believer would do 'greater works than these...because I go to the Father' (Jn 14:12). This last point has perplexed many, but surely it is true that in Christ's earthly ministry the Holy Spirit wrought through one body, one tongue, one mind, one heart, two hands, two feet. Christ foresaw the day when multitudes would be full of the Holy Spirit. The Spirit would then work through myriad bodies, tongues, minds, hearts, hands and feet. There would be a vast increase in the work. 'But', you say, 'Christ raised the dead, stilled the storm, multiplied the loaves and fishes.' I reply, Paul raised the dead! So did Peter! At various times in our day this has happened[1] as have miracles affecting food[2] and nature. Apart from recognizing the vast increase in numbers now being used by the Spirit, I share the expectation of many that outstanding miracles of power will become increasingly evident prior to the Lord's return.

Pentecost in Relation to Christ

There remain two further aspects to be considered. There is no direct reference by Christ in the gospels to the baptism in the Spirit apart from the promise He made after the resurrection:

> And behold, I send forth the promise of my Father upon you: but tarry ye in the city, until ye be clothed with power from on high (Lk 24:29).

It should, however, be noted that 'pentecostal' phenomena were very much in evidence in Christ's whole ministry— mighty miracles of healing, exorcism of demons, the raising of the dead, the commanding of nature, the operation of gifts of wisdom (as, for example, in the question of the tribute money) and the gift of knowledge (as in Christ's arrangements for the Last Supper). Faith, miracles, discernment and prophecy were wonderfully in evidence, and we read that He predicted:

And these signs shall follow them that believe: in my name shall they cast out devils; they shall speak with new tongues, they shall take up serpents, and if they drink any deadly thing, it shall in no wise hurt them; they shall lay hands on the sick, and they shall recover (Mk 16:17–18).

This last reference puts the stamp of Christ Himself on 'tongues', which will be the subject of later discussion in this work.

Finally, Christ Himself speaks quite categorically on resurrection ground about the baptism itself:

And, being assembled together with them, he charged them not to depart from Jerusalem, but to wait for the promise of the Father, which, said he, ye heard from me: for John indeed baptized with water; but ye shall be baptized with the Holy Ghost not many days hence. They therefore, when they were come together, asked him, saying, Lord, dost thou at this time restore the kingdom to Israel? And he said unto them, It is not for you to know times or seasons, which the Father hath set within his own authority. But ye shall receive power, when the Holy Ghost is come upon you: and ye shall be my witnesses both in Jerusalem, and in all Judaea and Samaria, and unto the uttermost part of the earth (Acts 1:4–8).

Careful students may have noted that Christ spoke increasingly of the Holy Spirit towards the end of His ministry, and on the very eve of His ascension the emphasis became unmistakably pointed. He 'charged' them not to depart from Jerusalem until they received the enduement of power. He did not suggest to them that this might be for their good or was one way to deepen their spiritual lives. Christ never made suggestions. He gave instructions. Similarly we never read of His expressing opinions. He made statements. In this case He did not even ask or simply encourage them to wait for this momentous event. He 'charged' them. In other words He gave a strict instruction. One cannot escape the conviction that this was a matter of extreme importance to Christ. Surely the truth is that He was keenly aware of the operation of the Spirit through Himself and He knew of the absolute necessity for the work of God that those who followed Him should operate under the same power. Note also he spoke of 'the promise of the Father' which He said 'ye heard from me'—so obviously He had referred to this previously.

His Last Words

Events move still nearer to the moment of His departure, and it is instructive to ponder His *last* words to His own. The last words of people going out of this world are often of great importance. In our own proverb it is said, 'Truth sits upon the lips of dying men.' With men of note, last words are perhaps particularly significant. I have often wondered what I would say, granted time and reasonable freedom from pain. I do not think I would reminisce about wonderful times in the past, nor about sentimental matters within a movement or congregation. Apart from farewells to loved ones I think my mind would be on the future—the growth and deepening of the work of God in so far as it has been committed to my hands. I would be anxious that high standards would be maintained, that God would be implicitly trusted, that prayer would be increasingly prominent, that gospel and pentecostal outreaches would be powerfully maintained, that our churches would be cared for and deepened in Christ, that leaders would exercise true authority, that individuals would not be neglected with the growth of numbers, that a cell system might be considered to help take care of this. I would charge those nearest to me to be faithful in the work as I would meet them one day. I would ask for total loyalty to Christ and unquestioning obedience to His commands. I think you will understand Christ. Was His mind not on the growth of His work? He said never a word about the miracles of the past, nor of the glorious fellowship the disciples had shared with him over the previous three years, nor of the Transfiguration—nor even of Gethsemane or Calvary itself. What did He say? 'But ye shall receive power, when the Holy Ghost is come upon you: and ye shall be my witnesses'. These are the last words of Christ, and immediately after we read: 'And when he had said these things, as they were looking, he was taken up; and a cloud received him out of their sight' (Acts 1:9). Surely we neglect His words at our peril. The receiving of the baptism of the Holy Spirit in the sense in which Christ spoke of it is a matter of tremendous seriousness.

Notes

[1] Study the life and work of Smith Wigglesworth.
[2] Read of the turning of water into wine in the recent Indonesian revival.

4

The Waiting Time— Ascension to Pentecost

A few days were to elapse between the ascension of Christ and the day of Pentecost, and it is good to review the position in which the disciples found themselves during those days and to look at the position into which they were to come. They had previously failed Christ desperately. They had all forsaken Him and fled in the dark hours. In spite of Peter's avowals of eternal loyalty and Christ's warning, Peter had broken. Surely there had come a moment when it was the hour of 'the power of darkness'. They had seen Him done to death and many, if not all, of their hopes had been buried with Him in a borrowed tomb. Note the poignancy of the words, 'We hoped that it was he which should redeem Israel' (Lk 24:21).

Suddenly He was alive again and the joy and the glory of it ran through their company like fire. The light returned. Joy and anticipation revived. Faith was restored. Victory and a sense of overcoming must have been upon them like strong wine. Surely they were ready to go. After all, they had witnessed the resurrection.

It is important to pause at this point and consider the position deeply: these were men who had journeyed with Christ, witnessed His miracles, heard His inner teaching, seen the multiplication of the loaves and fishes, seen the

dead raised and the storm stilled. They had known the
glory of His resurrection and stood with Him at His ascension. Who like them to spread His work?

Incapable Without the Baptism

Perchance one thing they had learned, as He lay buried in
the borrowed tomb—or rather when He rose from it, as He
had predicted—simply to believe what He said and obey
Him. I personally believe that they would be so ashamed
that they would be in a condition to believe every word He
uttered, and on certain matters He had left them in no
doubt. Surely He had said, 'Go into all the world and
preach the gospel' (Mk 16:15), and 'Make disciples of all the
nations' (Mt 28:19); but He had also said, 'Tarry ye in the
city, until ye be clothed with power from on high' (Lk
24:49). Quite simply these men, who had witnessed so
much, had known Christ so deeply, were considered quite
unable to fulfil their great commission without the baptism
in the Holy Spirit. They were to be radically affected. 'But
surely', you may say, 'some at least had known His power.
They had been out with the seventy and so great was their
impact on the kingdom of Satan that Christ could say He
beheld Satan as lightning falling from heaven. They had
healed the sick. They had cast out demons!' Yes, indeed!
But there was something critical still to happen within
them. Peter, James and John might have objected, 'Are we
not in a different position? We witnessed the Transfiguration and the agony in Gethsemane. Must we tarry too?'
'Indeed you must! There are no exceptions!' A radical event
was to take place. Neither the witnessing of the crucifixion,
nor the sensing of the power and glory of the resurrection,
nor being present at the ascension, was to effect it. One
thing, and one thing alone, was necessary: the enduement
of power from on high—the baptism of the Holy Spirit—
the experience of the day of Pentecost. 'Ye shall receive
power, when the Holy Ghost is come upon you'. 'Tarry'—

how long?—simply until it happens. The church today would be wise to heed the solemn injunction.

The Effect on Peter

And what is the effect to be upon them? Take the case of Peter. The man who had trembled and cursed before a servant maid is to be transformed. Fearlessly he is to accuse the assembled thousands in Jerusalem of the murder of Christ, and instead of being torn to pieces by the fanatical mob who had so lately committed that murder, he is to find fear falling upon them. They are to be 'pricked to the heart' and cry out for salvation and to turn to Christ by the thousand. What is to happen before this fulfilment? Peter is to be baptized in the Holy Spirit and in so being he is to be transformed. It reminds me of the word spoken of King Saul—'And the spirit of the Lord will come...upon thee, and thou...shalt be turned into another man' (1 Sam 10:6). This is precisely what happened to Peter and what happens in the outworking of a true baptism. This is how a man puts on Christ and becomes truly Christlike—not by his own effort, but by the transforming power of God within him. It is the ordained way of God. Not only does the baptism give power to witness for Christ, but it gives power to live above sin. This does not mean that we reach a place where it is impossible to sin, but we can reach a place, and indeed are responsible to reach a place, where it is possible not to sin.

It is difficult to over-emphasize the importance of the baptism, or the place which Christ gave to the ministry of the Spirit. Surely the whole record of the progress of the church of Christ is a record of the work of the Spirit. It is His work! It must be obvious that if even the apostles, who were so deeply privileged in knowing Christ personally, so deeply needed the baptism, Christians in our day have no less urgent a need.

And so to the day of Pentecost!

5

The Coming of the Spirit

And when the day of Pentecost was now come, they were all together in one place. And suddenly there came from heaven a sound as of the rushing of a mighty wind, and it filled all the house where they were sitting. And there appeared unto them tongues parting asunder, like as of fire; and it sat upon each one of them. And they were all filled with the Holy Spirit, and began to speak with other tongues, as the Spirit gave them utterance (Acts 2:1–4).

Christians are generally aware that Pentecost came fifty days after passover—but it is not so widely known that Pentecost fell on the anniversary of the coming of God on Sinai. A few scholars have noticed this, but the significance of the fact seems to have been almost completely overlooked.

There is an almost jubilant note in the description of the coming of the Spirit on the day of Pentecost, and surely those who tarried were in need of a jubilant note. They had been very deeply prepared. After the awful hours of Calvary, their own general defection, the dark days when He lay in the tomb, the surprised joy of resurrection, they were in no danger of taking the things of God lightly. Theirs had been a traumatic experience.

I have noticed in our day that Christians frequently seek the baptism in the Spirit much too lightly. They seem to

41

forget that an encounter with God is involved. They have not known the trauma which the early Christians experienced, and often come unprepared. In addition, salvation has frequently also been lightly presented and a knowledge of the holiness and majesty of God is too often lacking. In these circumstances, I have found in moving under the leading of God, the first sound that falls on their ears is not the jubilant note of Pentecost but the thunder of Sinai.

Sinai Related to Pentecost

It is wise for us to have a close look at the occasion of which Pentecost is the anniversary. In the epistle to the Hebrews we read:

> For ye are not come unto a mount that might be touched, and that burned with fire, and unto blackness, and darkness, and tempest, and the sound of a trumpet, and the voice of words; which voice they that heard intreated that no word more should be spoken unto them: for they could not endure that which was enjoined, If even a beast touch the mountain, it shall be stoned; and so fearful was the appearance, that Moses said, I exceedingly fear and quake (Heb 12:18–21).

When God came down on Sinai men fled from the base of the mountain. 'If even a beast touch the mountain, it shall be stoned; and so fearful was the appearance, that Moses said, I exceedingly fear and quake.' That mighty man of God was profoundly affected at the drawing near of God. Ponder this. By this time in his life Moses was already a seasoned vessel. He had been deeply used of God. He had been present when the bush burned with fire. At God's command he had appeared before the face of Pharaoh, working mighty signs and witnessing mighty miracles. He had led Israel over the Red Sea through divine intervention. He was no novice. Yet at Sinai this man was exceedingly afraid.

We have an almost immediate reaction as we read. We are glad that ours is the dispensation of Grace and not of Law. We sense the awfulness of the former and are relieved. One can almost hear the sigh of relief as the church goes on to read:

> For ye are not come unto a mount that might be touched, and that burned with fire, and unto blackness...

How thankful we are to be in the dispensation of Grace. With what pleasant sound come the words:

> But ye are come unto mount Zion, and unto the city of the living God, the heavenly Jerusalem, and to innumerable hosts of angels, to the general assembly and church of the firstborn who are enrolled in heaven, and to God the Judge of all, and to the spirits of just men made perfect, and to Jesus the mediator of a new covenant, and to the blood of sprinkling that speaketh better than that of Abel (Heb 12:22–4).

Yes. This is the position we know. We love the idea of drawing near to Zion and to the heavenly Jerusalem. It seems so lovely and comfortable and in keeping with our conception of a God of love. We may have only vague ideas about 'innumerable hosts of angels' and 'the spirits of just men made perfect' and pass quickly over the reference to 'God the Judge of all,' but surely we can rejoice in the idea of drawing near 'to Jesus the mediator of a new covenant, and to the blood of sprinkling that speaketh better than that of Abel.'

But then comes the shock. We go on to read:

> See that ye refuse not him that speaketh. For if they escaped not, when they refused him that warned them on earth, much more shall not we escape, who turn away from him that warneth from heaven: whose voice then shook the earth: but now he hath promised, saying, Yet once more will I make to tremble not the earth only, but also the heaven.

> And this word, Yet once more, signifieth the removing of
> those things that are shaken, as of things that have been
> made, that those things which are not shaken may remain
> (Heb 12:25–27).

Suddenly there comes the dawning awareness that the
interpretation may be wholly mistaken. It was a dreadful
thing to refuse the voice which warned from earth. The
voice now warns from heaven. 'Much more shall not we
escape, who turn away.' In that day the voice shook the
earth but now there is a promise to make tremble not only
earth but heaven. In short, it was a fearful thing to disobey
the voice that spoke from Sinai in the old dispensation; it is
a more fearful and dangerous thing to disobey the voice that
now speaks from heaven. Disobedient man is not now in a
more comfortable but in a much less comfortable position.
And in addition 'things shaken' will now be removed. There
will be judgment and destruction for refusing to obey the
voice that speaks in the dispensation of Grace. Gradually
we begin to realize something of the character of God. And
finally we read: 'Wherefore, receiving a kingdom that cannot be shaken, let us have grace, whereby we may offer
service well-pleasing to God with reverence and awe: for
our God is a consuming fire.' We should always remember
that while God is a God of pardoning grace and love, He is
still the God of Sinai. Do not let us imagine that there is any
change in His character or demands as we pass from the
dispensation of Law to the dispensation of Grace. Our
obligations become more rather than less exacting. Note
carefully that our service should be 'with reverence and
awe': there should be no light, frothy, casual, familiar
approach to God. 'Our God is a consuming fire.' Let us
ponder these words and ponder them deeply. This is the
God with Whom we have to do. Let us always remember
this as we approach Him.

This God came down on Sinai and men could not abide
His coming. The same God is to come down at Pentecost

and this time men do not flee in fear—but God comes right down and enters their very bodies. What has happened? What has made it possible? The cross has happened! They are clean by His blood and able to be filled with the Holy One. What kind of experience is this? Surely holy, awesome, glorious, terrible, and so with reverence and awe let us approach our Pentecost!

The Anticipation

On the day of Pentecost the company were gathered in obedience to the command of Christ and they had gathered specifically to receive the baptism of the Spirit, not to have general fellowship or hold a prayer meeting. They came for one purpose. Being human they almost certainly speculated as to what the experience would be like—how it would affect them. They were to be operated upon by God, and when we are about to undergo a surgical operation we are normally very interested indeed to learn about it. 'How long will I be under the anaesthetic? Will there be pain when I recover consciousness? How long will recovery take?' Etc. etc. We ask our medical friends, or others who have undergone the operation. Similarly we question those who have received the baptism about their experience. 'What did it feel like? How has it affected you?' But the first company of Christians had no such terms of reference. There was nobody to ask, for nobody had previously received. They waited for the unknown—but with perfect confidence. They knew it to be in the will of God. They probably had been anticipating it too after what Christ had said. They would have absolute faith. It had been promised by Him.

There are things for us to learn from this. Their seeking was *specific*. So ought ours to be. They were under instructions to 'tarry' until it happened. We too ought to tarry until it happens. They had total faith. We ought to have the same. I have noticed that people who come with this kind of attitude almost invariably receive very quickly. How wonderful to hear words like these: 'I believe God has promised me the baptism. I am sure it is for me and I don't intend to leave the room tonight until I receive.' So often such faith and commitment are honoured. The early disciples could not receive one day before the day of Pentecost—that was a point in history ordained of God for the first outpouring— but the window opened that day has never closed and men may now receive more or less at any time.

The Pentecostal Downpour

And suddenly there came a sound from heaven as of a mighty rushing wind, glory be! It is from heaven the sound comes. Note the word does not say that there came a wind. There came a sound, and I believe it was basically a spiritual sound which could be heard with human ears, and it was 'as the rushing of a mighty wind'. This sound is sometimes still heard. Two of my daughters were in an inter-denominational gathering some years ago where the Spirit began to move and a number of the company were to receive their baptisms soon after. From one side of the hall there came a distinctive sound—like a 'tingling wind moving through trees'. On the day of Pentecost the sound filled all the house where they were sitting, 'and there appeared unto them tongues parting asunder like as of fire'. The Authorised Version of the Bible speaks of 'cloven tongues' rather than of 'tongues parting asunder'. Some have suggested that this indicates 'speaking tongues'. The tongues were not described as tongues of fire but 'like as of fire'. The sound had been 'as of the rushing of a mighty wind'. The impression is clearly given of an attempt to convey things that were deeply spiritual in intellectual terms; likenesses are used which give a flavour but not the fulness of the experience. Similarly when asked to speak of the experience of the baptism people find it impossible to convey fully the feeling and the innerness of the experience. Some years ago I visited South America and tasted fruits I had never known before. I found it quite impossible to describe the taste to friends when I came home; there were no terms of reference, no similar tastes that I had ever experienced. I was unable to communicate my sensation. So on the day of Pentecost. It was not wind that blew. It was not fire that burned. The sound was like wind. The appearance was like fire. So with the baptism—it is indescribable. It has to be individually experienced to be understood.

Note that tongues are sometimes still seen in our day.

'And it sat upon each one of them'. Note the words carefully. There was a tongue above every head. There were no exceptions.

'And they were all filled with the Holy Spirit.' Again there were no exceptions.

Speaking in Tongues

They 'began to speak with other tongues, as the Spirit gave them utterance.' The first thing we read that they did on being filled is that 'they began to speak'. They became vocal. So ought we, in similar circumstances. Secondly, how did they begin to speak? They began to speak in other tongues. Who did the speaking? They did. We never read that God speaks in tongues. They did the speaking—but the Spirit gave the utterance. He supplied the power. And so it continues to our day.

Had I been asked in the first year after my baptism if it was essential for a person to speak in tongues to be fully baptized in the Holy Spirit I would probably have replied as follows: 'Something quite critical happened in me when my tongue was loosed. I had the feeling of a circle being complete. Power had come down from God and praise now went back up to Him and I had the knowledge of fulfilment and completion. Prior to that I had known love kindled and zeal born—but until that moment there was something not finished and it was something critical.' Even so, I would have said, 'But since the Bible does not categorically say that a person must speak in tongues to be baptized, I am not prepared to say it either.' I was not prepared to make my own case the foundation for a doctrine applying to all.

A year or two passed and something very significant occurred which deeply affected my ministry in relation to this matter. I had a strong urge to re-read Acts 2. I read and re-read and re-read it, and suddenly something became deeply imprinted on my consciousness. The symbol of the Holy Spirit on the day of Pentecost was not flaming hands to speak of working for God—nor flaming feet to run with the gospel—nor a flaming head to indicate thought—nor flaming shoulders to betoken burden bearing. It was not even a flaming heart to denote love. It was a flaming tongue, and what is the function of the tongue? Surely to speak: and this links with Acts 1: 'and ye shall be my witnesses both in Jerusalem, and in all Judaea and Samaria, and unto the uttermost part of the earth.' How does a man witness? Surely with the tongue.

I suddenly realized that the tongue might be a great deal more significant than I had realized. I knew that something significant had happened within me when I first spoke in tongues. It was like the opening of a sluice gate: a very small gate can hold back a veritable flood of water, and I found that water flowed abundantly. Such a small member—but what consequences of its being loosed of God! I now know that psychologists have recognized something of the importance of this part of our being—but I feel it was God Himself who gave me revelation that tongues were far more significant than I had previously realized. I am thankful for it. So often I have met people who have claimed the baptism without tongues, but in praying with them I have found that they were far from the experience. They may have had deep and glorious experiences in the Holy Spirit—there are, for example, anointings which are not the baptism—but such people can be in danger of not receiving their full birthright through lack of understanding.

It is important never to downgrade any experience in the Holy Spirit that any soul is privileged to have—but we must be careful not to misname such an experience lest we prevent such a person pressing on to receive the promise which is theirs from God—the promise of the baptism itself.

Finally I would point out that when the company came down from the upper room we do not read that anyone said, 'I had a wonderful experience of joy; so I know I must have been baptized in the Holy Spirit,' or others, 'I had a lovely warm feeling,' or 'I found a newborn zeal for God,' or 'I forgave all my enemies,' or 'I had a consecration experience,' or 'I was suddenly sanctified,' or even 'I had an immersion in the love of God.' I believe that any one or all of these things might have been experienced by one or other—but Scripture does not mention them. They all had *two* experiences in common which are mentioned. They were *all* filled with the Holy Spirit and they *all* spoke in tongues.

I indicated that the illumination of these truths deeply affected my ministry in a practical way. Since then I have expected all new converts to be baptized in the Holy Spirit and generally find this fulfilled. I also expect them all to speak in tongues and I am not aware that any have ever received without so doing—and the people concerned are numbered in thousands.

I must also mention, however, that I am aware of the fearful danger on the other side: of people thinking that by speaking a few words in tongues (often in imitation of others) they have received their whole birthright. Care must be exercised in both directions.

6

But What Are Tongues?

The question immediately arises: what are tongues? Reference has been noted in Mark 16:17–18 regarding signs which would follow 'them that believe'— 'they shall speak with new tongues'. Now we have come to the first actual fulfilment of this.

The question as to what tongues actually are is one which has occupied the minds of many and requires special attention.

In my own early days I was anxious to find unbiased truth and went to writers I felt would neither particularly favour a pentecostal viewpoint nor particularly oppose it. I searched the Encyclopedia Britannica and Chambers Encyclopoedia and Peake's Commentary, all of which I found helpful, and it may be that, almost half a century later, Peake's views will still be of interest. In discussing tongues and interpretations he wrote:

> unless the person who possesses the gift of tongues possesses also the power of interpretation, not only is what he says unintelligible to the hearers, but also to himself. It is indeed a religious exercise in which he is engaged, his spirit prays to God, but no ideas are conveyed to the mind of the speaker; it is all incoherent rhapsody so far as he is concerned, though probably Paul would have considered that the utterances did bear an intelligible meaning in themselves.[1]

And again, after discarding the views that the word 'tongue' might be taken in the physiological sense, or as referring to archaic language, he wrote:

> The actual utterances were probably such as we find in the magical texts, strings of words of strange formation and meaningless, but reminiscent of real, especially foreign, words. Possibly 1 Corinthians 13:1 pictures the form it (that is, speaking in tongues) took, 'not as a low-voiced stammering, but as shouting, sometimes dully resounding, sometimes piercing and shrill (Harnack). Similar phenomena...recur in revivalist and other movements; the Camisards and Irvingites are well-known examples (p. 648).

Thoughts from Norman Grubb

I remember being impressed too by Norman Grubb, son-in-law of C. T. Studd, and for long a leader of Worldwide Evangelization Crusade. He wrote of the baptism in the Spirit:

> This experience is pre-eminently a manifestation of the Spirit through the emotions. It is a presenting of the personality to God with such a complete abandonment and at such a pitch of intensity that the reason is finally transcended, the conscious being submerged, the love of God and the power of the Spirit flooding in through the whole range of the emotions.
>
> In this rational age, however, we are quick—and foolish—to despise and deride emotion. Such an experience as the above appears either ridiculous, unnecessary or excessive. Not so, indeed. For one thing, it was the experience of Pentecost, repeated on the historic occasion when the gospel was first preached to the Gentiles: it was common in the early church. Paul the rational, the master of logic, thanked God that he spoke with tongues more than them all! For another, the stirring of the emotions is the source of every human activity. No emotion as a driving force, no creative thought; no emotion, no great achievement; no emotion, no deeds of love nor exploits of faith. Love is largely compounded of emotion. God is love.

Therefore in stressing the baptism of the Holy Ghost with this sign following, the advocates of this teaching are penetrating to the most sensitive, most powerful chord in human nature, and are stirring their hearers to seek and find the living God through that avenue. The result is a people whose joy knows no bounds; fervent in testimony, free in prayer, large in heart, wide in generosity, with the warmth in their message and fellowship which attracts more hearers to their usually humble halls than probably any other denomination of equal size.[2]

The word translated 'tongue' comes from the Greek root 'glossa' which according to Strong, of concordance fame, means: 'The tongue', by implication a language (specifically one unacquired);—tongue.

In the Authorised Version the word 'unknown' is included before the word 'tongue' in italics. This is to indicate the nature of the 'tongue' but is not in the original text and is omitted by the revisers. Much has now been written about tongues and a fair measure of agreement exists among scholars as to their nature. Differences are more pronounced in the explanation of their value and present day relevance.

So What Are Scriptural Tongues?

It is not my purpose to deal exhaustively with this subject in this book. It may more appropriately be examined in detail in later studies on 'The Gifts of the Spirit'. It would perhaps suffice for the moment to quote extracts from something I wrote some thirty years ago:

What then are scriptural 'tongues'? Briefly they are an exercise of the human spirit under divine unction. They are a gift from God in a particular sense, and are not a merely natural function of any part of the human body or personality. In their utterance the individual concerned is conscious of divine anointing, exceptional clarity of vision, and a quickening of the mental processes. He is under no emotional strain, and has a sensation of being perhaps never more alive. He is completely conscious of what is happening, and is also conscious that he is not the initiator of that action. In themselves the tongues convey no meaning to his mind, although they benefit him spiritually. Nor do they convey meaning to the hearers unless these happen to be naturally familiar with the language used. Tongues are often used, and rightly, when none familiar with the language is present. If the utterance is in public it is for interpretation by one with the appropriate gift; if in private, it may be left uninterpreted. Tongues may, of course, be used to speak directly in foreign languages to foreigners and although there does not seem to be any scriptural instance of this recorded, there are modern instances.[3] In Acts 2 the understanding of tongues by Jews of the Dispersion seemed to be incidental. Those baptized were not speaking to them but to, or before, God. Whether a 'tongue' is always a foreign earthly language or not is doubtful. First Corinthians 13:1 might seem to suggest that angelic language may be used.

Whether a 'tongue' is always, or must necessarily be, a language at all, has been questioned. It cannot be denied that generally the benefits to be derived by the speaker from the exercise are not much, if at all, affected by whether it is so or not. It may be argued that the spirit is engaged in a spiritual function, and that whether what is spoken is understood, or capable of being understood naturally, is quite unimportant—interpretation being capable of bringing the utterance within the range of the understanding when necessary. There does not, however, seem to be any clear scriptural warrant for the view that something other than genuine language is used.

The scriptural uses of 'tongues' may be summarized as follows:

For Prayer: 'For if I pray in a tongue, my spirit prayeth, but my understanding is unfruitful' (1 Cor 14:14).

For Praise: 'I will sing with the spirit, and I will sing with the understanding also' (1 Cor 14:15). Here the word 'spirit' is equated with tongues.

For Personal Edification: 'He that speaketh in a tongue edifieth himself' (1 Cor 14:4).

For a Sign to Unbelievers: 'Wherefore tongues are for a sign...to the unbelieving' (1 Cor 14:22). Compare Mark 16:17–18: 'these signs shall follow them that believe...they shall speak in new tongues...they shall lay hands on the sick, and they shall recover.' Note that the Mark reference does not speak of the sign as exclusively for unbelievers.

For the Giving of Utterances Bearing Interpretation: 'He that speaketh in a tongue speaketh not unto men, but unto God' (1 Cor 14:2), the utterance being Godward. 'If I come unto you speaking with tongues, what shall I profit you, unless I speak to you either by way of revelation, or of knowledge, or of prophesying, or of teaching?' (1 Cor 14:6), the utterance being manward.

For a Sign of the Baptism in the Spirit: 'And they of the circumcision which believed were amazed, as many as came with Peter, because that on the Gentiles also was poured out the gift of the Holy Ghost. For they heard them speak in tongues' (Acts 10:45–6).

'But ye shall receive power, when the Holy Ghost is come upon you: and ye shall be my witnesses' (Acts 1:8).

Power! Witnesses! The key lies here. Those baptized were to carry the gospel. Without the baptism they were not equipped to fulfil their mission. The power was to enable them to witness. How were they to witness? With the tongue! By preaching! 'Go ye into all the world and preach the gospel'. Hence the symbol of the cloven tongue! Hence the fact that their every tongue was affected and set on fire! 'They all spake in tongues as the Spirit gave them utterance'.

Now what is the immediate effect upon an individual of first speaking in tongues? It causes a loosening of the organ, and a practical ability to allow it to be controlled by the felt power of the Holy Spirit. Not only is the mind illumined under the unction, but the actual organ of speech comes under direct control, although the human control is not thereby destroyed. It is as though a guiding hand is super-imposed upon a pilot's hand as he steers his craft. He can break the control. So the person speaking in tongues under God's control may break that control. Now it is much easier to allow God to control one's tongue in a language which the intellect does not understand, than it is to do so in one's own language, when the understood words are apt to dis-tract the mind and break the concentration. By learning the spiritual lesson through tongues, one is deepened and pre-pared for the reception of more important gifts of prophecy and interpretation and of inspired preaching. Tongues act as a kind of half-way house.

In view of the tremendous emphasis upon the tongue in this vital chapter (Acts 2) it would seem very dangerous to preach that baptism in the Spirit may be complete without the tongue being affected. Anointings and unctionings there may be, but is there not a part of the personality left undeveloped if the tongue remains unaffected?

Finally, if tongues are not sufficiently emphasized, there is a grave danger of seekers being cheated of their full inheritance through mistakenly accepting an incomplete experience as the full baptism. In my own case I was deeply moved by the Spirit and convinced that I had been bap-tized some hours before I first spoke in tongues, and it is significant that, when the latter occurred, it seemed as though the baptizing power had found the desired channel of expression. There was a feeling of completion with tongue utterance.

It should be underlined again for those who would dis-miss the spiritual gifts as ecstatic utterances, associated with a primitive state in the life of the church, that men like Paul were intellectual giants by any standard, and in any age. Yet such a man as he so strongly exhorts to seek such gifts, and values them so highly. He himself realized that his education, his intellectual brilliance, were as nothing compared with the unction and illumination of the Spirit. Many a time I have thanked God for having had the benefit of higher education and can, I trust, evaluate such things aright. The mind becomes a thousand-fold keener in the use of the gifts of the Spirit than in any merely natural function. The gifts 'rudimentary and primitive'?—rather the reverse—'illumined and mature'! There is a strange fallacy, popular with some, that the church of Corinth was a carnal unspiritual church, far behind the churches of many of our large denominations today. We regard ourselves as cultured now, educated, matured. One moment! In those days miracles were performed in the name of Christ, the sick were healed, the heathen were converted, the demon-possessed were liberated. In short, the works of Christ were wrought. Were churches in which, and through which, such things took place, inferior to what, in our day, have fast become declining social institutions? Do the lame now walk, do the wicked turn to righteousness? Too often not only are the ecstatic utterances ceased, the Life of Christ itself has largely, if not quite, departed and Christianity in some cases has been largely replaced by pseudo-morality and social custom. The fact that church members may on the whole be better educated than the early believers does not mean that they are better Christians—or, for that matter, Christians at all. Breadth or depth of learning is no substitute for holiness, and indeed is, in itself, quite useless in the things of God.[4] It is not, unless under divine control, a weapon or a glory in the kingdom at all. Holiness, not culture; goodness, not cleverness, are the hallmarks. If, in God's eyes, Corinth was carnal and, to a degree, carnal she was, may God help us! Since she had been so recently converted from heathenism she was liable to find that sin when it raised its head again could be horrible sin, not to be tolerated in our day. But as well as roughness, lack of experience, and immaturity, she had in her midst the priceless possession of the real power of the Spirit of God.

It is the writer's sober and considered conviction that

Corinth, although carnal from God's point of view, was in many ways both mature and advanced in comparison with many churches in our age. The supercilious, superior attitude which contemptuously looks down from modern heights upon carnal Corinth is lamentably mistaken.

Paul said, 'Forbid not to speak with tongues.' Let it be underlined. In view of the confusion in Corinth some possibly were so doing. In another case he had to instruct, 'Despise not prophesying'—probably again because abuse had brought the ministry of the gift somewhat into disrepute. The criticism must ever and only be applied to the abuse—never to the God-glorifying, man-edifying use. Paul said it. Who has countermanded the order? When did the practice cease? History tells us plainly—'Never!' We read of it in the following centuries: second, fourth, twelfth to fifteenth, seventeenth, eighteenth, nineteenth, twentieth. Irenaeus writes of it. Tertullian confirms it.

Augustine and Irenaeus

Augustine writes, 'We still do what the Apostles did when they laid hands on the Samaritans, and called down the Holy Spirit on them, in the laying on of hands. It is expected that converts should speak with new tongues.'[5] In our own day it is increasingly common. Millions now possess the gift. As never before, the Spirit is being outpoured upon all flesh. Surely the fulfilment of Joel's prediction is taking place as we approach the End Time. Praise God!

Miraculous phenomena continued long after the close of the canon of Scripture. Irenaeus (2nd century) wrote:

Even among the brethren frequently in a case of necessity, when a whole church united in much fasting and prayer, the spirit has returned to the ex-animated body, and the man was granted to the prayers of the saints...Some, indeed, most certainly and truly cast out demons. So that frequently those persons themselves that were cleansed from wicked spirits, believed and were received into the church. Others have the knowledge of things to come, as also visions and prophetic communications; others heal the sick by the imposition of hands, and restore them to health. And moreover, as we said above, even the dead have been raised, and continued with us many years. And why should we say more? It is impossible to tell the number of the gifts the church throughout the world received from God, and the deeds performed in the name of Jesus Christ.

As we hear many of the brethren in the church who have prophetic gifts, and who speak in all tongues through the Spirit, and who also bring to light the secret things of men for their benefit, and who expound the mysteries of God...[6]

A Man of Lewis

The following is a present day case and the inclusion of one such case seems not inappropriate in such a work. In the recent Lewis revival of world-wide fame, one of the most outstanding converts was a young man of Garrabost, with whom the writer is personally acquainted. After a period of deep conviction of sin, he was powerfully delivered and had a most remarkable vision. He felt himself more or less leaving the body, and in this state both distinctly saw and was spoken to by Christ. The voice was clear and unmistakable, and the place was filled with light. He did not realize at the time that all those present had not shared his experience and, being a young convert, he hesitated to speak—thinking that perhaps such things were quite common in Christian circles! Soon there came upon him a mighty baptism of the Spirit. Within twenty-four hours he was speaking in tongues. Without any expectation of it, without ever having the thought in his mind that there was such a thing, he almost literally 'bellowed out the unutterable gushings' of his heart. The language of Finney used earlier is peculiarly apt. Tongues, to my friend, were quite unknown and he had the impression, not so much of speaking, as of being spoken through. Never before had he heard them, nor had he been in contact with pentecostal people. Manifestly the experience was of God. Subsequently he has been much used in bringing deep blessing upon gatherings through his powerful gift of prayer; the Rev. Duncan Campbell of revival fame himself highly valued his ministry. The depth of his devotion to Christ and his passion for souls are alike remarkable. His testimony has borne witness to the genuineness of his experience. The change from a state of drunkenness to one of deep maturity in the things of God is an outstanding testimony to the power and faithfulness of a miracle-working God in a cynical age.

Notes

1 Arthur S. Peake, ed., *A Commentary on the Bible* (T. C. & E.C. Jack, 1920), pp. 647–8).

2 Norman Grubb, *The Law of Faith* (Lutterworth Press, 1947), p. 88.

3 Examples of this are cited from time to time in pentecostal reports. Some of the earliest to come to my attention were referred to in George Jeffreys, *Pentecostal Rays* (Elim Publishing, 1933). The appropriate extracts are quoted in Appendix 1 below.

4 C. S. Lewis commented, 'If you send a devil to Oxford you merely make him a clever devil.' He did not believe that education in itself made people better.

5 This quotation appears in Stanley H. Frodsham, *With Signs Following* (Gospel Publishing House, rev. ed.), p. 254, as well as in works by Carl Brumback and John L. Sherrill. No documentation, however, has been given in these works and it is only fair to mention that the authenticity has been challenged by A. A. Hoekema in *What about Tongue-Speaking?* (Paternoster Press, 1966), pp. 16–17. In a more verifiable source Augustine describes the exceedingly loud, 'wordless' voice of the congregation in response to news of one of the miracles he records (*The City of God, xxii.* 8).

6 Quoted in *Pentecostal Rays*, p. 195.

7

The Human Response

Now there were dwelling at Jerusalem Jews, devout men,
from every nation under heaven. And when this sound was
heard, the multitude came together, and were confounded,
because that every man heard them speaking in his own
language. And they were all amazed and marvelled, saying,
Behold, are not all these which speak Galileans? And how
hear we, every man in our own language, wherein we were
born? Parthians and Medes and Elamites, and the dwellers
in Mesopotamia, in Judaea and Cappadocia, in Pontus and
Asia, in Phrygia and Pamphylia, in Egypt and the parts of
Libya about Cyrene, and sojourners from Rome, both Jews
and proselytes, Cretans and Arabians, we do hear them
speaking in our tongues the mighty works of God. And they
were all amazed, and were perplexed, saying one to another,
What meaneth this? But others mocking said, They are
filled with new wine (Acts 2:5–13).

In Jerusalem

I n the previous chapter we have seen something of the
effect of the coming of the Spirit on the followers of
Christ. We now come to the reaction of the multitude
who came crowding around the upper room as a result of
the sound they heard. Precisely what this sound was Scripture does not make clear. It could have been the sound 'as
of a rushing mighty wind' or it could have been the sound

made as the disciples spoke in tongues. In my view it was the latter.

The feast of Pentecost drew great crowds of people annually to Jerusalem and the people referred to here were Jews of the Dispersion. In earlier times their forefathers had gone into captivity or for other reasons left Palestine. They had, however, retained their Jewish identity and religion. Many had been born in other lands and learned the languages of their adopted countries. They also, of course, knew Hebrew, the language of their fathers. These with home-born Jews formed the multitude which surrounded the upper room.

The account is amazing. People of such a wide range of nationalities suddenly heard Galileans speaking in the languages with which they were familiar through living in foreign parts. What precisely happened? The people baptized began to speak in tongues. They spoke words which were quite meaningless to them. To understand this, I would direct attention to 1 Corinthians 14:2 where we read, 'For he that speaketh in a tongue speaketh not unto men, but unto God; for no man understandeth; but in the spirit he speaketh mysteries.' And we further read, 'Wherefore let him that speaketh in a tongue pray that he may interpret. For if I pray in a tongue, my spirit prayeth, but my understanding is unfruitful' (vv. 13–14). This means that a person speaking in tongues does not speak to men but to God. He does not understand what he says, nor does anyone else unless what he says is interpreted. Nevertheless he himself is edified. This shows that there is a means of communication with God which bypasses the human intellect. (This, incidentally, was one of the first considerations which drew me to Pentecost. I reasoned that if there was a need of the human spirit for this in the first century there must be the same need now.)

As the disciples on the day of Pentecost were filled with the Spirit and spoke out in tongues, no doubt with great joy and power, the words would be quite unfamiliar and meaningless to them—but extremely meaningful to those who understood naturally what was being said (and not in this case by interpretation). They could say, 'we do hear them speaking in our tongues the mighty works of God'. Perhaps a more recent experience of a similar kind will help to clarify the matter.

And in Congo

Some years ago I heard, at different times and separately, from the late Mr William Burton and the late Mr James Salter, co-founders of the Congo Evangelistic Mission, of the initial downpouring of the Holy Spirit in baptism on their early Congo believers. Evidently they had gone through a very trying time and indeed had come to a point where they were meeting the people for the last time. They were going home. Mr Salter's grave had been dug at least twice. In later days a converted witch doctor was to ask: 'Why is it that poison which kills a black man does not kill a white man?' 'Why? What do you mean?' 'Well, we put enough poison in your food in the early days to kill seven black men and you were not even ill!' 'If they drink any deadly thing it shall in no wise hurt them,' was surely fulfilled.

However, an end had come—they thought! That night awful conviction came upon the Africans. God moved in great power and the Holy Spirit was outpoured. There were, in fact, about a hundred and twenty present and they began to be baptized in the Holy Spirit. My friends could testify: 'We went round and listened to the people as they were being baptized and heard them use sounds which Lubans normally cannot make. We heard them speak in English, German and perfect Parisian French.' (About eight languages were listed.) They spoke of the birth and the life of Christ, of His death and Resurrection and particularly of His coming again—a doctrine, I seem to recollect, with which they were not familiar at that time. A work of God was born that night and hundreds of thousands, if not millions, will be in the glory one day as a result. In later days powerful revival was to sweep the Congo Field. These early missionaries were men who knew the miraculous, divine provision, mighty healings and glorious deliverances.

What happened in Congo that night very closely resembled what happened in Jerusalem on the day of Pentecost. It should be noted that in both cases the miracle was a miracle of speaking—not one of hearing—as some have wrongly suggested about Pentecost.

On the day of Pentecost there were three reactions and two distinct groups of people: amazement and perplexity on the part of the Jews of the Dispersion and mockery from the home-dwellers—the men of Judea who said, 'They are filled with new wine.'

To deal with the last point Peter with the eleven rose to their feet. And so to the first sermon of the church age.

8

Peter's Sermon

But Peter, standing up with the eleven, lifted up his voice, and spake forth unto them, saying, Ye men of Judaea, and all ye that dwell at Jerusalem, be this known unto you, and give ear unto my words. For these are not drunken, as ye suppose; seeing it is but the third hour of the day; but this is that which hath been spoken by the prophet Joel; And it shall be in the last days, saith God, I will pour forth of my Spirit upon all flesh: and your sons and your daughters shall prophesy, and your young men shall see visions, and your old men shall dream dreams: Yea and on my servants and on my handmaidens in those days will I pour forth of my Spirit; and they shall prophesy. And I will show wonders in the heaven above, and signs on the earth beneath; blood, and fire, and vapour of smoke: the sun shall be turned into darkness, and the moon into blood, before the day of the Lord come, that great and notable day: and it shall be, that whosoever shall call on the name of the Lord shall be saved (Acts 2:14–21).

To the Mockers

Note again that there were two sections in the crowd—the Jews of the Dispersion and the Jews of Judea and Jerusalem. The first had been mightily impressed by what they had seen and heard. They were in the presence of the miraculous and supernatural. They knew something very unusual had happened. The words they heard the Galileans speak were meaningful and the very fact of the use of the words was in itself beyond their understanding. These men were far from mockery. The local Jews, however, were of a cynical mind and it was to them that Peter addressed himself. He first precisely identifies them. 'Ye men of Judaea, and all ye that dwell at Jerusalem, be this known unto you, and give ear unto my words.' Another writer has noted, with a trace of humour, that the first sermon of our dispensation commences with a denial by Peter that he and his friends are drunk, and as supporting evidence says, 'seeing it is but the third hour of the day'—in short, it is too early in the day to be drunk. How far removed is the scene from many of our latter day services with all our meticulous control and formality. It is probable that people had been prostrate on the floor, as those baptized often are, and that they were unsteady on their feet. These people had been filled, not with new wine, but with the wine of heaven. The power of God was mighty and men would find it difficult to contain it. Glory be! We could well do with such divine disturbance. Our traditions might be somewhat upset, but how glorious would the consequences be!

Fulfilment of Prophecy

Peter goes on to indicate that what has happened is the fulfilment of the prophecy of Joel, and some points should be particularly noted.

The same chapter of Joel which contains the prophecy quoted also states: 'for he giveth you the former rain in just measure, and he causeth to come down for you the rain, the former rain and the latter rain, in the first month'.

The Jews were familiar with the fact that the former rain was required for the germination of the seed in spring time. The latter had to fall to bring fulness to the crop before reaping. Similarly it seems that the rain of the Holy Spirit came on Pentecost for the planting and watering of the young church. We expect that it will come in flood-tide power before the harvest is finally gathered. The prophecy of the outpouring began to be fulfilled on the day of Pentecost. Its final fulfilment is still future—but many feel that we are at least at the foothills of the last mountain range. Surely it is true that for every hundred people baptized in the early days there are thousands now. I do not think it an exaggeration to suggest that there are over fifty million people alive now who have been baptized in the Spirit.

The promise of the outpouring was categoric and unconditional. Some of the promises of God are deeply qualified, for example:

> Bring ye the whole tithe into the storehouse, that there may be meat in mine house, and prove me now herewith, saith the LORD of hosts, if I will not open you the windows of heaven, and pour you out a blessing, that there shall not be room enough to receive it (Mal 3:10).

In other words: if we fulfil our part God will fulfil His promise. In this case, however, the promise is quite unconditional. He did not say: 'If Christians get together and agree amongst themselves I will do this thing,' or 'If the major denominations are of one mind,' or 'If the professors of theology in the universities of the world get together and agree about the matter then I will open the windows of heaven and pour you out this blessing.' No. He said, 'in the last days I will pour forth of my Spirit'. This is wonderful. It is something which is happening, and which will happen, and no man will prevent it. A man may try and stand as Canute is reputed to have stood in the waves declaring: 'Come no further—' but still the tide came in. This river which flows from the throne of God will still flow and deepen as it flows. A man may try to stem its flood and be thrown on the bank like driftwood. A movement may stand against it and be broken and divided—but still that river will flow on. Men are wise to get into its flood and be borne along by it. A vast outpouring is inevitable. It will surely come.

We read, 'your sons and daughters shall prophesy'. Note that there were women in the upper room as mentioned in Acts 1:14. In this scripture they are envisaged as prophesying and again we read: 'Yea and on my servants and on my handmaidens in those days will I pour forth of my Spirit; and they shall prophesy' (Acts 2:18). In a day when God is so deeply using women, and when there is so much controversy about their ministry, these verses should be noted.

The prophecy goes on to speak about signs and wonders with astronomic phenomena. This should be compared with Matthew 24:29–31. It is clear that before the return of Christ, which is the day of the Lord referred to in Acts 2:20, there will be not only an outpouring of the Spirit but the occurrence of remarkable phenomena. Nor will that coming be private and secret—but glorious and public—but why 'the great and terrible day of the Lord'? The day of the coming of Christ to those of us who know Him will be one of joy and glory but to the unsaved it will be a dreadful day— a terrible day—the day of the Lord.

From time to time report comes of various types of phenomena—particularly in association with revival. In my own experience something once occurred which made the coming of Christ and His control of events in that hour more understandable than had formerly been the case.

A Heavenly Vision

I had been teaching Pentecost in an area many years ago where there was little knowledge of the baptism. Many were filled but there came a point where the work was deeply resisted and was indeed in danger of being quenched. At the critical hour when I feared the boat was going down, I sat with one other after three of our friends had left the gathering. No word was spoken. I sat in despondency. Suddenly there was the sound of running feet. It was long past midnight and the three ladies who had recently left returned. They came back into the room—but they could not speak. Quite literally they were unable to speak. I said, 'What is wrong? Has somebody run after you?' Ultimately one said, 'There is a man out there. He is in white.' I said, 'I am going out to see.' A second said, 'It is Christ.' Never shall I forget the emotion of the moment. Gradually we got the story. They had been walking along the pavement when suddenly one of them noticed a strange band of light against a very dark sky. One of her friends gripped her arm and said, 'Do you see that?' 'Yes,' she said, 'I have been watching it.' They stood still and the band of light formed a cross of light in the sky and out from it came a luminous cloud. The face and figure of Christ formed and He seemed to lean forward. They said, 'We went prostrate on the pavement.' And one added, 'We could not look again for the power and the glory.' 'Well,' I said, 'I am going out.' And we all went out. I did not see Christ. The vision had gone—but I did witness astronomic phenomena for hours that night—balls of light swinging near the horizon. I spontaneously prophesied and one of the remarkable objective things is that there were physical effects on my body for about a fortnight afterwards. One of the three ladies was a recent convert. Another had been baptized in the Spirit just shortly before and the third had had a deep consecration experience earlier that night and was to be baptized a few nights later—an occasion on which she testified to this experience. That was a remarkable night as she lay prostrate at the feet of a critic of pentecostal experience, singing in glorious new tongues and for a long time quite unable to speak a word in her own language. Many others were baptized around that time.

One of the consequences of the earlier night of vision for me was this: previously I used to wonder what would happen to cars, trains and planes when Christ came. Would they run out of control when believing drivers were caught up to meet the Lord? I have never again been concerned. So great was the feeling of divine control that night as a little corner of earth came under heaven's power that I have no doubt that His control in the hour of His coming will be over all. The prospect is glorious.

Salvation and the Birthright

Peter in his sermon then proceeds to preach the gospel. He is a transformed man and—instead of standing in fear before the servant maid—he accuses the assembled thousands of the murder of the Christ. His words are terrible and powerful and—instead of producing a wrath culminating in an attack upon his person—the hearers are 'pricked to the heart' and ask what they should do. They are shown the way of salvation and promised the gift of the Holy Spirit.

The next part is particularly significant. It was the outpouring of the Holy Spirit which had drawn the people together. Peter in verse 32 had said of Christ:

> This Jesus did God raise up, whereof we all are witnesses. Being therefore by the right hand of God exalted, and having received of the Father the promise of the Holy Ghost, he hath poured forth this, which ye see and hear.

Now the promise is to them. Peter speaking of the gift of the Holy Spirit said, 'For to you is the promise, and to your children, and to all that are afar off, even as many as the Lord our God shall call unto him' (v. 39). This is rich—the promise of the outpoured Spirit, or in other words the promise of the baptism, is to that generation and to their children, that is the next generation, and to how many more?—'even to as many as the Lord our God shall call'. That takes us right down to our day and right to the end of the dispensation. To be called into the Kingdom is the criterion for being eligible for the baptism. The birthright is for us every one.

Birthrights are interesting things, and most people with natural birthrights and inheritances are anxious to get all of this world's goods to which they are entitled. My father and an uncle were in partnership in a farm. My father had a large family and my uncle none. Now it was my uncle's intention to leave his share of the farm to our family, but he died of a heart attack on his way to sign his will. This let in a great number of others—I had over one hundred cousins on this side of the family—and I well remember learning much of human nature in those days. A valuation was disputed and redone. There was greed and lust for money. It was horrible—but it was natural.

In later days, long after I had become a deeply committed Christian a relative from whom I had not expected to receive anything died and I discovered that one thirteenth of his estate was to come to me. A dwelling house comprised part of that estate—a house I passed frequently. Suddenly I was interested in that house. What condition was it in? How much was it worth? The normal reaction of humanity to a birthright or an inheritance is not, 'Must I have it?' but rather, 'How much and how soon?' Sadly in the spiritual world many seem indifferent to their birthright. We hear the questions 'Is it necessary to have a second experience? Have you got to speak in tongues?' rather than 'Is it possible for even me to receive? May I also be privileged to speak in tongues?'

And the Fear of the Lord

And what was the result of the outpouring of the Holy Spirit and the preaching of Peter under His power? About three thousand souls were saved and, note, 'Fear came upon every soul.' There is today a great ignorance about the value of fear. There are two types of fear. There is a fear which is harmful and is cast out by perfect love, but there is a fear of the Lord which is the beginning of wisdom. The first fear can be paralysing and extremely harmful. Indeed, frequently deliverance is required to deal with demons of fear. I remember one young man who on being delivered said, 'I feel free of fear for the first time in my life.' My co-leader, Miss Elizabeth Taylor, had discerned the spirit and described it as gigantic and grotesque—looming over him, having been there for a lifetime. Never shall I forget the words, 'The sword of Christ is now in your heart.' Immediately the demon was affected and it was like the deflation of a balloon as the young man was set free. Frequently those afflicted with spirits of fear will run out of meetings when the presence of God is strong but they are often ultimately set free. I have found that this kind is not amongst the most difficult to put out.

But what of the other fear—'the fear of the Lord, which is the beginning of wisdom'—the fear that is associated with reverence and awe? Note the place of fear in the lives of Jacob and the apostle John. Jacob sware by the fear of his father Isaac. One day he saw a ladder going up to heaven and the angels of God going up and down on it and said, 'This is a fearful place—this is none other than the house of God. This is the gate of heaven.' John referred to himself as the disciple whom Jesus loved. He seemed to be in a very close relationship to Him and it was he who leaned on His breast at the last supper. But note—when this same John saw Him in ascension glory, when he was in the Spirit on the Lord's Day, on the isle of Patmos, he fell at His feet as one dead. We often think we will go into heaven in a very homely, casual way. We will not. As we draw near to God or He draws near to us there will be an awe. I have found that in that area of spiritual experience in which we live, and with which we have grown familiar, there may not remain the sharp awareness of godly fear and awe—but in the moment we are drawn into a new and nearer place with God, there is a shrinking of the flesh and the emotion of fear. At the sharp edge of this kind of contact we should expect such a reaction. The old carnal for ever draws away from the divine. The new man is irresistibly drawn on into the fulness of life.

9

The Five Cases

In the New Testament we read of the baptism in the Spirit actually being received on five occasions: on the day of Pentecost, and in the cases of the Samaritans, Paul, Cornelius and his household, and the Ephesian twelve. On two occasions the Spirit is spontaneously outpoured. On three He is received by the laying on of hands. On three occasions all spoke in tongues, while on a fourth, in Paul's case, we are not specifically told if he spoke in tongues at the time of his baptism but we are told later that he spoke in tongues more than all the Corinthians. In the remaining case, that of the Samaritans, we are not told whether they spoke in tongues or did not—but we are told that Simon Magus saw that through the laying on of hands the Spirit was given and he himself desired a like ability to lay on hands. In short there was an outer evidence of the inner experience the Samaritans received. In no case is the experience equated with salvation. It is always viewed as a separate and distinct experience—sometimes occurring near to salvation in point of time, sometimes considerably later.

The five cases are so instructive that they should be considered individually. The first, the day of Pentecost, has been dealt with. The second is that of the Samaritans.

The Samaritans

In the eighth chapter of Acts we read:

> Now when the apostles which were at Jerusalem heard that
> Samaria had received the word of God, they sent unto them
> Peter and John: who, when they were come down, prayed
> for them, that they might receive the Holy Ghost: for as yet
> he was fallen upon none of them; only they had been bap-
> tized into the name of the Lord Jesus. Then laid they their
> hands on them, and they received the Holy Ghost. Now
> when Simon saw that through the laying on of the apostles'
> hands the Holy Ghost was given, he offered them money,
> saying, Give me also this power, that on whomsoever I lay
> my hands, he may receive the Holy Ghost. But Peter said
> unto him, Thy silver perish with thee, because thou hast
> thought to obtain the gift of God with money. Thou hast
> neither part nor lot in this matter: for thy heart is not right
> before God. Repent therefore of this thy wickedness, and
> pray the Lord, if perhaps the thought of thy heart shall be
> forgiven thee. For I see that thou art in the gall of bitterness
> and in the bond of iniquity. And Simon answered and said,
> Pray ye for me to the Lord, that none of the things which ye
> have spoken come upon me (Acts 8:14–24).

Peter and John prayed specifically that the Samaritans
might receive the baptism of the Holy Spirit. They had
been converted under the preaching of Philip and while
many miracles had taken place they had not received the
Holy Spirit. For a long period in the past there had been
friction between Jerusalem and Samaria on their relative
positions, and it may be that God was now making Samaria
dependent upon Jerusalem in the receiving of the Holy
Spirit lest the old division should remain. In any case the
Spirit came with the laying on of hands. We note that
Simon, the former sorcerer, saw that through the laying on
of hands the Spirit was given. The question immediately
arises, 'What did he see?' We are not told, but we are at
least left with the knowledge that an effect of the baptism
was evident. It was not simply a 'faith' experience with no

outer evidence. It was something so significant that Simon offered money to receive the ability to produce the miracle. Note again that the experience of baptism came after salvation.

Paul

The next case is that of Paul:

> And Ananias departed, and entered into the house; and laying his hands on him said, Brother Saul, the Lord, even Jesus, who appeared unto thee in the way which thou camest, hath sent me, that thou mayest receive thy sight, and be filled with the Holy Ghost. And straightway there fell from his eyes as it were scales, and he received his sight; and he arose and was baptized; and he took food and was strengthened (Acts 9:17–19).

Converted on the Damascus road, Paul went in his blindness to a house in Damascus. There under the ministry of Ananias he received his sight and was filled with the Holy Spirit and baptized in water. Salvation and the baptism in the Spirit are separated in time and the latter is by the laying on of hands. Tongues are not mentioned. We should note, however, that in his first letter to the Corinthians in later days, Paul could say, 'I speak with tongues more than you all' (1 Cor 14:18). He did not say, 'I used to speak in tongues when I was young in the things of God and immature,' but 'I speak' (present tense) or 'I go on speaking in tongues more than you all'. In 1 Corinthians 13:11 he said, 'When I was a child, I spake as a child, I felt as a child, I thought as a child: now that I am become a man, I have put away childish things.' This Paul, this mature apostle, continued to speak in tongues, letting us see clearly that it pertained to his maturity in Christ—not his childhood. A quotation from Dean Farrar is of interest in this connection:

Paul, as he stands in the light of history; Paul, as he is preserved for us in the records of Christianity; Paul, energetic as Peter and contemplative as John. Paul, the hero of unselfishness; Paul, mighty champion of spiritual freedom. Paul, greater preacher than Chrysostom, a greater missionary than Xavier, a greater reformer than Luther, a greater theologian than St Thomas Aquinium. Paul, the inspired Apostle of the Gentiles, the servant of the Lord Jesus.

This is the man who said, 'I thank God that I speak in tongues more than you all.' This is very instructive.

Cornelius

The next case is that of Cornelius:

> While Peter yet spake these words, the Holy Ghost fell on all them which heard the word. And they of the circumcision which believed were amazed, as many as came with Peter, because that on the Gentiles also was poured out the gift of the Holy Ghost. For they heard them speak with tongues, and magnify God. Then answered Peter, Can any man forbid the water, that these should not be baptized, which have received the Holy Ghost as well as we? And he commanded them to be baptized in the name of Jesus Christ. Then prayed they him to tarry certain days (Acts 10:44–8).

This is an amazing case. Peter had been miraculously sent to speak to Cornelius and his household. Cornelius had been miraculously prepared for his coming. Peter, to his considerable surprise and in spite of his initial reluctance, finds himself preaching the way of salvation to a Gentile audience. The word is received and the Holy Spirit outpoured. Without any laying on of hands, He came, and it would appear that He came immediately on the reception of the word. The two experiences do not become one, but little time seems to have elapsed between them. The next part is very significant. 'They of the circumcision' (that is, the Jews who came with Peter) were amazed, because the gift of the Holy Spirit was poured out on the Gentiles. Now the next part should be particularly noted: 'For they heard them speak with tongues, and magnify God.' We never read that speaking in tongues is the only evidence of the baptism in the Holy Spirit, but the evidence contained in this verse is the only evidence that Scripture itself cites as evidence of the baptism. The significance of this should not be lost. Remember the prejudices against the Gentiles. God met these prejudices in an unanswerable fashion. There could be no question of the salvation of Cornelius and his household. The Holy Spirit was poured out and this was a clear outward evidence of the fact. Tongues here are of great significance as being in themselves an evidence of the baptism.

The Ephesian Twelve

This leaves the fifth and final case—that of the Ephesian twelve:

> And it came to pass, that, while Apollos was at Corinth, Paul having passed through the upper country came to Ephesus, and found certain disciples: and he said unto them, Did ye receive the Holy Ghost when ye believed? And they said unto him, Nay, we did not so much as hear whether the Holy Ghost was given. And he said, Into what then were ye baptized? And they said, Into John's baptism. And Paul said, John baptized with the baptism of repentance, saying unto the people, that they should believe on him which should come after him, that is, on Jesus. And when they heard this, they were baptized into the name of the Lord Jesus. And when Paul had laid his hands upon them, the Holy Ghost came on them; and they spake with tongues, and prophesied. And they were in all about twelve men (Acts 19:1–7).

This case deserves almost a chapter of this book to itself and should be considered in some detail.

Paul found in Ephesus a group of about twelve men whom he took to be disciples of Christ. To these men he put a question which many readers may consider strange. 'Did ye receive the Holy Spirit when ye believed?' We do not know why he asked the question. He may have become suspicious as he listened to their conversation or their prayers. We are just not told what triggered the enquiry— but the question itself speaks volumes. First, it implies that a person can be a believer on Christ without having received the Holy Spirit (in the baptismal sense). We would never, for example, dream of asking a person, 'Were you saved when you believed on Christ?' To be saved is to believe on Christ, and to believe on Christ is to be saved. Or again, we would not say, 'Did Christ receive you when you were born again?' If you were born again Christ received you. If you were received by Christ you were born again. But not so with salvation and the baptism. It is evident that a person could have one without the other and that Paul recognized this.

Their reply is also very illuminating: 'Nay, we did not so much as hear whether the Holy Ghost was given,' or, as another version renders it, 'We have not so much as heard whether there be any Holy Ghost.' Immediately Paul would be suspicious. He well knew that the formula for Christian baptism in water was into the name of the Father, Son and Holy Spirit. Any person so baptized was bound to know of the existence of the Holy Spirit. Thus he questioned, 'Into what then were ye baptized?' It then emerged that they had been baptized with John's baptism. So often at this point the opponents of Pentecost exclaim with delight, 'That explains it! These men were not really Christians when Paul met them!' That does not, however, get round the implications of the question which Paul asked them—nor does it weaken the case for Pentecost which the next events so strongly establish. Paul took them and baptized them with Christian baptism. Now, no individual in the New Testament is ever baptized in water to make him or her a Christian. People were baptized in water on profession of their faith in Christ. Baptism in water is a post-salvation experience and is only for those with such an experience. Thus, when these men went under the waters of baptism they were Christians in our definition of the term. When they stood dripping on the banks of the river, in what way were they different from many Christians in our day—who have believed on Christ and been baptized in water—but who have still not been baptized in the Holy Spirit? How did Paul treat them? Did he say, 'Now, brethren, you have received your birthright. Accept by faith that you have received the baptism of the Holy Spirit'? No, indeed! Nor did he say, 'If you had been present in the upper room on the day of Pentecost, or if you had been with me in Damascus when Ananias laid hands on me, or had you been with the Samaritans when Peter and John laid hands on them, or with Cornelius and his household when Peter preached, you would have had a wonderful experience of power—but you need no longer expect such a manifestation. It is now nineteen years after Pentecost;* so go on your way rejoicing.' No such thing. He laid hands upon them and the Holy Ghost came on them and they spake with tongues and prophesied.

This is a remarkable incident. In earlier days it was sometimes argued that the baptism was accompanied with tongues at 'beginning' times—Pentecost being the beginning for the church, the Acts 8 occasion the beginning for the Samaritans, and similarly Acts 10 for the Gentiles; Paul's could be regarded as a special case. But thank God for Acts 19! It is the beginning of nothing in particular. Paul simply comes on a company whom at first he took to be disciples but who were in fact in an irregular position for New Testament saints, and he proceeded to regularize the position. Thus he shows the position the church should be in relative to this matter. One feels he would do exactly the same today across the face of the world were he here in

---

* According to Scofield's reckoning.

person. May I ask the reader the question sincerely and in no controversial spirit, 'Have you received the Holy Spirit since you believed and, if you have not, in what way is your position any different from those believers' before Paul's hands came upon them—if you too have been saved and baptized in water?'

I indicated at the beginning of this section that this case is particularly significant. I have been preaching Pentecost for about forty years and frequently meet opposition, and sometimes from scholarly people. Many of the old simplistic arguments against Pentecost have been abandoned but opposition still remains. Never, might I say, throughout the years have I known an opponent able to get off the hook of Acts 19. I do not suggest that I am a particularly able exponent of the truth, but the argument is so strong that a third rate advocate could go into court confident of winning the case.

It seems to me that the evidence of Scripture is unanswerable. The evidence of history is on the same side and in our own day the evidence is further borne out in experience across the world.

10

Other Relevant Matters

I t is not the purpose of this book to go into the detail of all the pentecostal phenomena which are mentioned in the New Testament—or to examine the 'gifts' of the Spirit in detail. Suffice perhaps to mention that from the day of Pentecost onwards the miraculous intervention of God in human affairs was both expected and experienced. The Acts of the Apostles might be more properly named the Acts of the Holy Spirit. Thousands turned to Christ; the sick were healed; the dead were raised; prison doors were opened; angelic ministry was experienced. Evidence is abundant and unanswerable. Powerful gifts of the Spirit were in operation.

Gifts of the Spirit

Nine of the gifts are listed in 1 Corinthians 12:8–11:

> For to one is given through the Spirit the word of wisdom; and to another the word of knowledge, according to the same Spirit: to another faith, in the same Spirit; and to another gifts of healings, in the one Spirit; and to another workings of miracles; and to another prophecy; and to another discernings of spirits: to another divers kinds of tongues; and to another the interpretation of tongues: but

all these worketh the one and the same Spirit, dividing to each one severally even as he will.

Some have suggested that the miraculous was associated with the foundation of the church and should not be expected to continue. The history of revival, of course, shows that with Christians in a right relationship with God the miraculous recurs again and again. As Wesley said:

> It does not appear that these extraordinary gifts of the Holy Spirit were common in the Church for more than two or three centuries...The cause of this was not as has been vulgarly supposed because there is no more occasion for them; because all the world were becoming Christian. This is a miserable mistake.... The real cause was: the love of many, almost all Christians, so-called, was waxed cold.[1]

There is evidence that not only the miraculous in general, but tongues and other gifts of the Spirit, were in operation in various ages between Pentecost and the twentieth century.

To argue that such could be expected to cease with the completion of the canon of Scripture, or that experiences such as baptism in the Spirit recorded in early days should no longer continue, is peculiarly foolish. We would not say that the new birth was necessary at the beginning, but after a generation had experienced it their children should no longer look for such a life-changing experience; they are born into it; they should accept that it is theirs. This would be condemned, and rightly condemned, as deadly heresy. We say Scripture shows clearly that the new birth is essential for every child of Adam's race and similarly that the baptism of the Spirit is the birthright of every believer. Indeed the doctrine of Pentecost is as clear in the New Testament as the doctrine of salvation. It is not founded on a few obscure and difficult texts, but runs like a shining highway throughout the Book.

To.....es to Continue

'But', som..... objects, 'surely Paul said tongues will cease.' At this the opp.....nts of Pentecost once rejoiced and rubbed their hands. 'The..., they argued, 'Paul said it, tongues were to cease'—failin.... observe that prophecy and knowledge were also to pass aw.... When was this to happen? In Paul's day? No! When? 'W...n that which is perfect is come'. The beginning of 1 Cor.thians 13 is wonderfully supportive of Pentecost. Tongues with prophecy, miracles, faith and other highly desirable things are seen in relation to love as precious stones in a cluster, surrounding a diamond. Tongues are included in wonderful company—thus highlighting rather than detracting from the gift. In the later part of the chapter the wording should be carefully noted:

> Love never faileth: but whether there be prophecies, they shall be done away; whether there be tongues, they shall cease; whether there be knowledge, it shall be done away. For we know in part, and we prophesy in part: but when that which is perfect is come, that which is in part shall be done away. When I was a child, I spake as a child, I felt as a child, I thought as a child: now that I am become a man, I have put away childish things. For now we see in a mirror, darkly; but then face to face: now I know in part; but then shall I know even as also I have been known (1 Cor 13:8–12).

Thus as long as knowledge (in the acquired sense) continues, tongues may be expected so to do. In the age to come knowledge will be of an unlearned type, intuitive and spontaneous—'we shall know as we are known'. This will happen when we see 'face to face'—that is, in the eternal age. Thus tongues may be expected to remain until then. The fact that the mature apostle who had long since put away childish things continued to use them has already been noted.

Baptized into One Body

There remain two scriptures which oppon⸙⸙⸙ of the views expressed in this book frequently quote⸙

> For in one Spirit were we all baptized into one body, whether Jews or Greeks, whethⸯ bond or free; and were all made to drink of one Spirit (1 Cor 12:13).

This is taken to refer to the baptism in the Spirit, but why is this so? Outright opponents of Pentecost who know Christ teach that the Spirit is received at salvation and that that is an end of it. Many who teach that there is a later experiencing of the fulness also hold that the baptism, being an initiating experience, is really received at salvation, and it is its fulness or realization which comes later. Many in this school obviously know from experience that something of profound significance happens after salvation—often long after—but they experience theological difficulty in viewing this as baptism in the light of the earlier salvation experience.

I have never been fully able to understand the difficulty. Surely Scripture teaches that the new birth is by the operation of the Spirit. A person at salvation is sealed by the Spirit. At that moment he 'receives' the Spirit in one sense of that word. (Remember the words of Christ, 'he abideth with you, and shall be in you.') In the scripture under review the baptism described is not baptism in the Spirit but baptism into the Body of Christ. He, the Spirit, is the baptizer. In the baptism in the Spirit it is Christ who is the baptizer as John predicted earlier. Baptism is an initiating experience—baptism in water symbolizes the beginning of a new life. Baptism in the Spirit was to give a new empowering. Neither was to be repeated.

There may be many fillings of the Spirit but one baptism only. Baptism in water was not a repeatable experience either. Nor is a man twice baptized into the Body. 'But', you may still object, 'the wording of 1 Corinthians 12:13 is ambiguous and I am not convinced that it does not refer to the baptism in the Spirit.' Suppose for one moment that it does: that would then mean that the baptism of the Spirit was common to all believers—for surely all believers are in the Body. If this is so we must find another name for the experiences which Paul, the believers in the upper room, the Ephesian twelve, Cornelius and his household and the Samaritans had—since they were already Christians, and in the Body, when the Holy Spirit came on them in a very particular way. Surely to interpret 1 Corinthians 12:13 in the second way creates more problems than it solves and by no means removes the difficulties of those opposing the view that the baptism is a separate experience distinct from salvation.

Readers should note further amplification of this point in the Question and Answer section (chap. 12) below.

Do All Speak in Tongues?

The second problem verse also comes from 1 Corinthians 12. Verse 30 reads: 'Do all speak with tongues? Do all interpret?'

The answer expected here is obviously, 'No.' Paul is thus seen as agreeing that New Testament Christians did not all speak in tongues, nor were they expected to do so. Now since all Christians were expected to be baptized in the Spirit it is argued that it must be possible to be baptized in the Spirit without speaking in tongues. But is this necessarily correct?

Early exponents of pentecostal doctrine frequently drew a distinction between the sign of tongues ('These signs shall follow them that believe', and again, 'wherefore tongues are for a sign') and the gift of tongues. The first they associated with initial speaking at the time of the baptism—which might be repeated in similar meetings—not interpreted, nor expected to be interpreted, as on the day of Pentecost. The gift of tongues, on the other hand, was viewed as something received either at the baptism or later when an individual received the ability to give utterances in tongues which were interpreted in public gatherings. I have never felt that this distinction beween sign and gift could be fully logically substantiated. It seems to me that a gift in use was a 'sign' to the unbeliever—but I do know from experience that many who speak in tongues initially at baptism do not go on to give utterances bearing interpretation—and before some do, something quite particular happens. They speak of a particular action of the Spirit upon them: is this 'something' the receiving of a gift? Now it was certainly the tongues which bore interpretation to which Paul refers in 1 Corinthians 12:30. If the foregoing is correct the difficulty is resolved.

While I have felt it right through most of a lifetime of ministry to emphasize the importance of tongues, I am anxious never to over-emphasize this. I felt, as I indicated earlier, that God Himself indicated to me something of the significance of the tongue in Acts chapter two. The symbol of the downcoming Spirit was a 'tongue'. The disciples were to be witnesses; it is with the tongue that a person witnesses. Their tongues were to be set on fire by God. Now we learn from 1 Corinthians 14 that tongues can be like a halfway house to prophecy, and the interpretation of tongues is equivalent to prophecy. In the case of the Ephesian twelve, we read, 'And when Paul had laid his hands upon them, the Holy Ghost came on them; and they spake with tongues, and prophesied' (Acts 19:6). If true prophecy accompanied the experience rather than tongues, I would not deny that the baptism had taken place. If I am correct in this, no difficulty with 1 Corinthians 12:30 remains. I would, however, have to be convinced that the prophecy was indeed prophecy.

Not all, I know, will accept this. Nor am I anxious to gloss over difficulty. It is better to be scrupulous in these matters and attempt to 'divide the word of truth' honestly. At the end one surveys the whole field and takes all the evidence into account, with the leading that the Holy Spirit Himself has given.

A Revelation from God

I think I will end this section with an incident from earlier life. Many years ago as a comparatively young man, I found myself on the Isle of Lewis. I was there clearly at the call of God and had known His voice, as clearly as though audible. He moved in great power and many were baptized in the Spirit. There came, however, a day when I was very strongly opposed. Anti-pentecostal influences had come from the South, and some will remember from earlier days the contempt which accompanied the expression 'tongues people', applied to pentecostals—as though such were a lesser breed and certainly a group to be viewed with great suspicion. My spirit was deeply discouraged on a particular day. I was due to preach at night—but I felt that Satan was really tormenting me. 'These tongues people,' was reverberating in my mind. Suddenly God drew near and I was reminded that if Paul could come back and join me that night he too would be a 'tongues' man. He would come over and sit beside me. It then struck me that if the rest of the apostles could be present they too would all be over on my side of the house. I was feeling much less lonely at that point and then it struck me—it really struck me—that if the whole of the New Testament church could be there that night they would almost all be over beside me. The room was far too small! My opponents were now a very small minority and, I trust it won't seem ungracious of me to say, an insignificant minority (from one point of view). The glory rose in my soul and I exulted in God my Saviour. I have very faithful friends who scan the drafts of this book and at the slightest evidence of my enjoying a victory in what they consider an inappropriate way they take the offending words right out. But this I did enjoy, and my joy I have decided to share. Oh, yes, I realized that day as never before that the New Testament is pentecostal literature written by pentecostal writers to pentecostal people. To be a Christian was almost synonymous with being pentecostal. The power of the Lord came that night and I have never been lonely in that sense again—nor ever been assaulted in that particular way either. God dealt Satan a blow that day on that point from which he had no recovery. Is it wrong of me to say, 'And I enjoyed it!'?

Note

[1] Jeffreys, *Pentecostal Rays*, p. 205.

11

A Personal Testimony

Over the years I have probably asked hundreds if not thousands of people to testify to their experience of the baptism in the Holy Spirit and strangely enough have seldom given an account of my own. And yet I think that my experience, both of salvation and the baptism, is rather unusual. I feel that in a book of this type it may be of value.

Searching for Christ

I was born into a Christian family and from earliest days knew of the necessity of salvation. In the circles in which I moved there was a great emphasis on 'believing' and little emphasis on the need for conviction of sin. Indeed the connection between finding Christ and turning away from sin almost entirely escaped me. I did not find Christ in early days although I intensely longed to 'be saved'. During one illness I was deeply disturbed. The reality of eternity came on me. I found no place of rest and indeed, I knew terror. I resolved that, if I recovered, I would not rest until I found Christ and could be assured that in health or sickness all was well with my soul. Then commenced a period of real turbulence. In secondary school I met scientific views and criticism of Scripture which troubled me intellectually. I found myself in a position where I profoundly believed in hell but could not find Christ. I felt I ought to love Him— but found that I did not. In fact, there was something about Him that disturbed me and I was not comfortable at the thought of being in His presence. I came to a point, and this lasted for about two years, when I feared I had committed the unpardonable sin and was in a desperate condition. Night after night I endured agony and knew what it was for my whole body to shake with the fear of hell. Some of the experiences of Bunyan described in *Grace Abounding* I understand so well. I sought help from leaders and preachers— but often to no avail. They told me to believe in Christ, but generally did not tell me what this meant. 'Believe that He died for your sins'—but I could not believe. I so much wanted to, but I had no assurance. I then began to read carefully and discovered that believing in Christ normally meant believing in His Messiahship—believing that He was the Son of God. I noticed, too, that for a Jew to recognize His Messiahship immediately meant that he became His follower. Still there was no rest.

Then one day, in exasperation, a faithful counsellor asked what nobody else had ever really asked before: 'Is there sin in your life that you are not giving up?' Indeed there was—but never before had I realized that this might affect my salvation. I was startled—but at least a door of hope was opened. Another counsellor, a good man, once asked me, on hearing of some of my difficulties, 'When did God last speak to you?' 'Well,' I said, 'I read such-and-such in this verse and such-and-such in that verse.' 'That', he said, 'is not what I mean. When did God last speak to you?' I suddenly became aware that I did not know that I had ever heard God speaking to me in the sense he meant. This too I stored in my mind. A third and earlier counsellor treated me in such a way as to make me, throughout a lifetime, considerate of other souls in difficulty. 'I am not going to help you. Far too much is done for young people today. They get things on a plate that we had to strive for and they don't appreciate them. Go and find out for yourself.' I departed with the tears running down my face—for I was in deep despair. The man was a leader in Christian work and in one way he may have done me good: I learned never to treat anybody else in such a way. So I found myself still unsaved but with an inkling that a right attitude to living might make a difference to my being received of God, and there was no price that I knew of that I would not have paid to find Christ. By this time I was getting to the senior stages of secondary school and many of the intellectual doubts remained unresolved. But then a lovely thing happened. It may be that others have come by the way God opened to me, but if so, I have not met them.

The Place of Joy

I was a keen student of literature and had a deep love of poetry. I had also read widely in Christian biography. Suddenly I realized that true joy is a remarkably rare quality. I had noticed a sadness, almost a depression, over so much of literature and poetry. So often the poet brings 'the eternal note of sadness in'. Joy, I felt, was not to be found in this aesthetic field—much as I loved this field. Sadness, yes! And a grieving for lost yesterdays, yes! But joy—real, deep joy, satisfaction, fulfilment, hope—no! Now I had noticed that this kind of joy was found in the lives of Christians who lived deeply sacrificial lives—men like Hudson Taylor, founder of the China Inland Mission; C. T. Studd, founder of Worldwide Evangelization Crusade; and George Müller, founder of the Bristol Orphanages. It seemed to me that the catechism was correct when it said, 'Man's chief end is to glorify God and enjoy Him for ever.' That should be true, full enjoyment. Something deep within me was persuaded that man should be joyful. I cannot rationalize it. I cannot explain it. I was deeply sure it was true. I observed that the only place I had met it was in the lives of Christians of the type mentioned. I further argued that the religion which produced this quality of life must be true and real. My intellectual problems passed like a cloud of the night. There remained only the moral problem. One day the crisis came and I decided before God that whether He ever took me or not, whether I was ever saved or not, from that hour I would live to the best of my ability as a Christian should. I was prepared to live for ever, if necessary, at the gate of heaven, waiting. I would live for God. Within about one hour the light broke on me and I knew I had passed from death to life. The invitation came: 'Come unto Me all ye that labour and are heavy laden and I will give you rest.' I had heard it before, but I was able to respond that day and I believed that He had received me. I had His word for it: 'He that cometh unto me I will in no wise cast out.' My soul found peace.

Moral Choices

Before ending my testimony to salvation I would like to stress again the connection between a right attitude to God and sin before being received of God. I have observed many times that souls have had very costly moral choices to make before they find Christ. So clearly I remember a young soldier about to be demobilized, who was deeply affected under gospel preaching. He wanted to decide for Christ, but he wanted to postpone the decision. 'You see,' he said, 'the boys are having a party next Friday night and I want to go.' He knew well that there would be activities inconsistent with a Christian stand. He wanted to be one of the boys. Christ could come later. I warned him seriously against the thing which he planned but still made arrangements to meet him after his party. The hour came and, as I expected, passed—with no meeting—no salvation. It so often happens. 'Go thy way for this time,' said Felix to Paul, 'and when I have a convenient season, I will call thee unto me.' He never did. There was no more convenient time. Paul he left in chains. No decision for Christ was made, and this despite the fact that earlier he had literally trembled under Paul's preaching.

Finally, on this point, remember Pilate to whom Christ said in the judgment hall, 'Every one that is of the truth heareth my voice.' 'What', Pilate asked Christ, 'is truth?' Elsewhere Christ had said, 'He that willeth to do my will shall know of the teaching.' In other words, 'Pilate, if you are a true man you will believe in me.' Pilate did a very dangerous thing that day. He seemingly sought truth and almost immediately he was to be faced with it most disconcertingly. He may not have known that Christ was the Son of God but he did know that Christ was an innocent person. As the Jewish leaders brought pressure to bear on him, he realized that he would run a great risk if he set Jesus free. His political position hung by a thread. There had been previous insurrections. Another complaint to Caesar could have dire consequences—particularly if it looked as though he had set free a man who was founding a kingdom. 'If you set this man free, you are not Caesar's friend,' bayed the pack. Pilate saw the truth and hated it. It was a simple truth, 'The man before you is an innocent man.' It did not suit. What a choice lay before Pilate. See the high drama of the hour. Christ stands arraigned at the tribunal of man to be judged of him. Draw back the curtain and you will see Pilate the judge himself weighed on the balances of God. Pilate made his choice. He called for a basin and washed his hands not in innocency, as one put it, but in blood. All the world knows that Christ suffered under Pontius Pilate. Pilate might have set Christ free and fallen from Caesar's favour, but been remembered for ever as a man of integrity and a man of character. I believe he would have been a man who would also have found Christ. As it was he delivered Him to be crucified—and went out by one door to eventual disgrace and banishment from Rome by the very Caesar whom he feared to offend and ultimately, if tradition is correct, to a suicide's grave in southern Italy. Christ, on the other hand, went out another door, by way of Calvary, resurrection and ascension to sit down on the right hand of God. Man may have judged God but God also judged man, and so much for man depended on a right moral choice. Frequently a clear-cut moral choice lies close to the door of salvation. The Holy Spirit often presses such a point and so should a counsellor. Never make salvation cheap. Never expect it to be cheap. A man who has no intention of repenting and giving up sin is not received of God. A right choice and the intention to give up sin do not save him but are often necessary prerequisites of salvation. And so to the baptism in the Spirit.

Early Interest in Pentecost

My first interest in Pentecost goes back a long way. As a boy I had come across a book which contained Charles G. Finney's description of his own baptism in the Spirit and this had an extraordinay effect on me. It produced a holy awe and indeed a fear. Yet it had a fascinating quality too. I felt I had seen truth which could never again be unseen, and although the Christian group with which I was associated strongly held the view that the Holy Spirit is received at conversion, I knew that there was something more than what most Christians experienced at that time. So significant was Finney's account that I am including it here:

> I received a mighty baptism of the Holy Spirit. Without any expectation of it, without ever having the thought in my mind that there was any such thing for me, without any memory of ever hearing the thing mentioned by any person in the world, the Holy Spirit descended upon me in a manner that seemed to go through me, body and soul. I could feel the impression, like a wave of electricity, going through and through me. Indeed it seemed to come in waves of liquid love, for I could not express it in any other way. It seemed like the very breath of God. I can remember distinctly that it seemed to fan me, like immense wings.
>
> No words can express the wonderful love that was spread

abroad in my heart. I wept aloud with joy and love. I almost literally bellowed out the unutterable gushings of my heart.[1]

A few years passed which found me keen to win others for Christ, learn more about the Bible and work for God generally. At an earlier stage I had met a pentecostal lady who chatted to me about 'tongues'. Although I was then still a schoolboy, I was studiously inclined and was so interested that I began to read around the subject in the Bible. I found 1 Corinthians 14 very difficult to understand, nor was it greatly illumined when I went for help to my spiritual leaders. I remember one of them, at a late stage in developments, making the classic comment: 'Peter', he said, 'wrote of Paul's epistles, "wherein are some things hard to be understood, which the ignorant and unstedfast wrest, as they do also the other scriptures, unto their own destruction." ' For him 1 Corinthians 14 seemed to fall into this category! Another leader did, however, give me good advice. He was a humble and godly man. He said, 'Young man, I do not understand this scripture, but you will find if you leave things in God's hands he will reveal all you ever need to know.' Too often people who do not know pretend to knowledge and do harm in counselling. This man was truly humble and I found his advice remarkably sound throughout a lifetime. Still unsatisfied I continued to probe.

Confession of Sin

Then there came a critical point which focused my attention directly on the baptism in the Spirit. Norman Grubb's biography of C. T. Studd was serialized in the *Christian Herald*. In this I found that Studd openly preached the baptism as a second experience and an essential one. This, he taught, should be received by faith. My group did not accept this teaching and I was left pondering. I became totally convinced that there was something else for me. The terms were not clearly defined in my mind. Tongues were not an issue but there came on me a tremendous draw to a closer walk with God—full consecration—sanctification—and I tried to receive by faith! My efforts were largely in vain. Then God began to speak to me. He did not say, 'I am pleased that you are seeking Me. This brings joy to My heart. You will become really useful in My Kingdom.' Nothing like that at all. As I look back, it is as though He said two words only: *Sin* and *Confess*.

The truth is that I had taken a very wrong step some time prior to this and while it had not killed my spiritual life it lay beween God and me. I wanted to move on and get closer to God. God wanted the hidden sin brought out into the light. As I opened my Bible hoping to read of consecration and communion with God, I saw nothing but confess, confess, confess! It was unmistakable and I knew I had to go through with it. At great cost I did and the experience became a foundation of my life. In it a great deal of pride was dealt with and as I paid the price I found that Christ Himself drew near and I knew Him as I had never known Him before. One of the wonderful sustaining words He gave was, 'He will temper the wind to the shorn lamb,' and He did. I cannot easily over-emphasize the importance of this experience. Often we seek God's power when God is seeking our holiness. Sin was the initial barrier between man and God and again and again it raises its head, and God will have none of it. Any man who will go on with God must be prepared to have sin dealt with radically.

And Its Results

Immediately things began to happen. I knew Christ then—really knew Him as a Person beloved. I think it was about this point that there came a tremendous desire in me to gather people and preach the gospel. Looking back I feel that these were genuine stirrings and gave a pointer to things to come. But God was still preparing me. My interest in Pentecost deepened further as I became acquainted with a pentecostal family. The mother, a lady over sixty, was deeply spiritual and I used to question her again and again about inner things until one night she used a strange expression which had a critical effect on me. It may be that she had become exasperated at my endless questions. In any event she said, 'I wish you would come up here some night to tell me you were drenched with the Spirit.' I had never heard the term 'drenched with the Spirit' before and it gripped me.

The Attraction of Tongues

At the beginning of this chapter I indicated that, on the intellectual side, my way of coming to Christ was unusual; and so was my coming to the baptism in the Spirit. Through the years I have noticed again and again that 'tongues' have been a stumbling block to enquirers. 'What', they say, 'is the use of tongues? I don't understand "tongues"! Have I got to speak in tongues?' etc. etc. For a long time I felt that as personal salvation was the cross of the evangelicals, so 'tongues' was the cross of the pentecostal movement. My case was radically different. As I indicated earlier, 1 Corinthians 14:2 fascinated me. Together with verses 4 and 14 it revealed that a person speaking in tongues did not speak to men but to God, that he did not himself understand what he said, that his mind was in fact barren but even so his spirit was edified. This clearly must mean that there was a spiritual means of communication with God which bypassed the intellect, and the whole process was an edifying one. I argued further that if there was a need for this in the beginning of the dispensation there could be no less a need for it in our day, since the need is a need of the human spirit. I came as a student to Pentecost being totally convinced intellectually of the need of 'tongues'—without either having ever heard them or having ever been in a pentecostal meeting.

Crisis Hours

So I made my way home with the words 'drenched in the Spirit' ringing in my ears. That night I made a vital decision. 'I am going to ask God for this experience if it is for me and if I don't receive it I am not going to worry.' I was very objective. My emotions were not involved. I had no intention of working myself up to a certain type of psychological state or of giving myself a merely psychological experience. Before retiring to bed I knelt at the kitchen fire and prayed, 'O God, if there is a baptism in the Holy Spirit or a filling with the Holy Spirit for me which I have not as yet received, I pray that I may receive it now, if it be Thy will, for the Lord Jesus Christ's sake. Amen.' (The exact words I remember because they were very carefully chosen.)

There were plenty of conditions and qualifications in that prayer. I did not want to get mixed up over semantics. I did not want to ask for something God might not want to give or had really already given. I was not totally sure about my request. I prayed and waited for a short time and went to bed. For about four nights I prayed the same prayer and at first nothing happened. About the third night, however, I felt a cleansing experience beginning although I was under no particular teaching on this at the time. I resolved to have nothing to do with known wrong things but I was prepared to let everything of a doubtful nature go too—and actually there was a doubtful thing. Looking back I recognize it now as having been dangerously wrong. I was also prepared to let anything go which God might further reveal. God had undoubtedly come to clean the ground. On the fourth night, my wife was obviously going to be some time in the kitchen. On the earlier evenings she had been in bed while I 'tarried'. So I decided that I could just as easily tarry in bed. This I did. I prayed the same prayer and nothing particular happened, and then suddenly something did happen and it was something quite unexpected! I found myself becoming very irritated—almost irrationally irritated—over a very natural matter. There seemed perfect justification for my annoyance and as soon as my wife came in I was minded to express it. Indeed I think I was on the point of getting up so to do when it was as though a voice spoke to me: 'Are you more concerned about expressing your irritation than you are about going on seeking Me for this experience?' Immediately I was stopped in my tracks and turned and sought God. The next stages were critical. I remember going over in my mind the verses from 1 John 4:

> Beloved, believe not every spirit, but prove the spirits, whether they are of God...Hereby know ye the Spirit of God: every spirit which confesseth that Jesus Christ is come in the flesh is of God: and every spirit which confesseth not Jesus is not of God.

and from 1 Corinthians 12:

> Wherefore I give you to understand, that no man speaking in the Spirit of God saith, Jesus is anathema; and no man can say, Jesus is Lord, but in the Holy Spirit.

The First Shower

I went over His deity. Yes, I believed He was not only the Son of God but God the Son. I went over my own identification with Him in conversion. As you will see I was being very careful—and suddenly something happened. My whole breathing had deepened. I had not done this. It had happened and I had the sensation of going out of the body and being somewhere above it—without a twinge of fear. By this time the bed was beginning to shake and I said to my wife, who had come in, 'Don't be afraid if I begin to speak in tongues!' Poor soul! I had not told her a word about my seeking the baptism and I don't know that I had ever spoken of 'tongues'. I tend to be very private about deep things that are moving in my soul, at least in their beginnings. As it happens, I did not speak in tongues that night but I did experience a remarkable sensation of warmth and joy. Power flowed through me, right down my arms, and both my hands tingled. I found a new love for God. I really loved Him, and a zeal for Him was born that night. I rose in glory in the morning and felt I had been baptized in the Holy Spirit. I felt as though wave upon wave of life was welling up from deep within. I was tremendously happy.

The Deluge

A few days passed and I found myself in a group in the home of the lady who had expressed the hope that I would be 'drenched in the Spirit'. We were gathered at my behest for a Bible study on 1 Corinthians 14. This group had never gathered before and comprised pentecostal and Brethren believers. I found to my consternation that the pentecostal folk were not as well instructed in doctrine as I had expected (and ever after I have sought to teach people to know the doctrines they hold and know their scriptural foundations). The time came to 10:50 p.m. (it is strange how such details imprint themselves on the memory!) and we were about to go home when I asked if we could have prayer before dispersing. We knelt down (we seemed to kneel more in those days than people do now) and, as is normal in pentecostal circles, some of the folks began to speak in tongues in an undertone. Now I had never heard tongues. I had never been in a pentecostal meeting—so I had no preconceived ideas as to what might happen—but I did find that the undertone gave me a wonderful cover to speak quietly to God myself. I began to quote that beautiful poem of Myers:

Who that one moment has the least descried Him,
   Dimly and faintly, hidden and afar,
Doth not despise all excellence beside Him,
   Pleasures and powers that are not and that are:—

Ay, amid all men bear himself thereafter
   Smit with a solemn and a sweet surprise,
Dumb to their scorn and turning on their laughter
   Only the dominance of earnest eyes?

Yea thro' life, death, thro' sorrow and thro' sinning
   He shall suffice me, for He hath sufficed:
Christ is the end, for Christ was the beginning,
   Christ the beginning, for the end is Christ.

I was part way through the poem when suddenly I became aware of a tremendous power in the room above me—don't ask me how I became aware; I cannot tell in normal intellectual ways—but I knew with an absolute knowledge that it was so. I was not thrown on to the floor but gently went prostrate. It was the only position which seemed appropriate. The Power came into me— tumultuous, wonderful, awful, glorious. Like Finney I felt that I almost literally bellowed out the unutterable gushings of my heart. It must have been very loud—and I was a quiet person. I was right out of myself and I believe in that hour I received my call to preach. I envisaged it there and it has been completely fulfilled. The power to do it came then. Still all was not complete. The power was, as I said, tumultuous—as though seeking avenues of expression which were still not open. Someone, soon followed by others, came over and laid hands on me saying, 'Just let the Lord take your tongue, brother.' To me these words were quite meaningless but my mind must have gone to one word outwith the language, which I spoke. Immediately there came a whole stream of tongues—free-flowing and lovely. I had a wonderful feeling of completion. It was as though the downcoming power had found the desired avenue of expression and flowed freely back up to God. How

long I remained there I cannot say, but the moment came
when we all got up. I remember a young lady saying, 'Well,
you will be happy now.' 'No,' I said, 'I am not happy.
"Happy" does not describe my feeling. I am too deeply
moved for happiness.' I felt I had been moved to the depths
of my being—indeed to depths I had not previously realized existed within. I was profoundly awed. I had encountered the divine.

Maintaining the Level

I remember another member of the group saying, 'Oh, I
remember my baptism. I walked on air for about three
weeks—but your feet will come down again.' I said nothing
but I inwardly resolved that, by the grace of God, my feet
would not come down. They have, from time to time, but I
have never accepted that the 'down' position is God's normal. We should live in the 'up' position and as soon as we
go down we should get back up as quickly as possible. I
once almost drowned as a boy but found that the river
bottom was a wonderful place from which to launch myself
upwards to where I could break surface and cry for help. So
it should be in the spiritual life.

   It is important to have a right attitude to these things.
We often get what we expect. If we accept a low level of
living as our birthright, this is what we will be apt to attain.
If we think that we should live as overcomers, this too is
likely to be achieved. I remember noticing that two revivals
were going on in Africa at the same time—the Rwanda
revival and one experienced by the Congo Evangelistic
Mission. The leaders of the first considered that 'revival'
ought to be the normal condition of the church and for
decades the revival continued. CEM leaders, on the other
hand, looked on revival as a blessing which came upon men
from time to time in the sovereignty of God. They did not
look on it as something which would be continuous and
indeed they received as they expected. In time it did pass.

A Negative Reaction

I remember a third reaction that night. One individual who had never been in such a gathering was deeply shocked and so far as I know never took a step towards Pentecost. He had come, I think, quite unprepared and I doubt if he has ever again attended such a gathering. I have often wondered about him. Some time before this we had compared spiritual experiences and had both lamented the fact that at weekly communion we had again and again had to confess to God our failure and wrongdoing. We agreed that it became difficult to go through the same process so regularly. We were both sincere, and both recognized failure— but neither of us knew the way out. In Pentecost I found it. I discovered that there came a power which enabled me not only to witness but also to live in victory. It did not mean that I attained a place where sin was impossible, but I did find a place where it was possible not to sin. Arrows which at one time would have pierced right through seemed to meet invisible armour and fall to the ground. It was quite wonderful to find a real power whereby sin could be successfully resisted. I do not know if my friend ever found victory.

Lasting Consequences

And what of the consequences of the experience? God alone can assess that. I know that the power that came on me on that glorious night began to be manifest in preaching and later in ministering to others for the baptism. It came for healing, exorcism and other spiritual operations. Thousands have found salvation, thousands been baptized in the Spirit and many healed and delivered. How has this happened? Not by anything of man—but by the power of God alone.

In case there are any who find it difficult to understand the language re the coming of the power of God, let me make it plain that the power is often felt, literally felt, on the physical body. Sometimes, and as it was in my case at the beginning, the body may shake with the power. Later as the vessel becomes seasoned the physical manifestations tend to pass but the reality of the power remains. The power is frequently felt power.

Quite literally, from the hour of my baptism, life changed. I entered a dimension that had only been dreamed of before. The New Testament I found to be true: not only in theory but in practice. God was real and His promises true. There was no disappointment.

Points to Ponder

There are five things related to my baptism to which I would like to draw attention:

1) *The Need for Cleansing*. Sin must be put away. Again and again I find this in dealing with others. It is not a matter which should be lightly passed over.

2) *The Laying on of Hands*. When hands were laid on me, I felt that one person was doing me harm. It may be that his life was not right. I have never forgotten this and strongly counsel people never to lay on hands casually because others are doing it, and particularly not to do it if they are themselves out of touch with God. Laying on of hands is a ministry and should only be practised by those who have the calling. Some time after my own baptism I fell into the custom prevalent in many pentecostal circles in those days where all and sundry laid on hands and not only for the baptism but for many other things. Various and sometimes differing instructions would be given, and often in loud voices. Many a seeker must have found things very difficult. One day a close and faithful friend came to me and said, 'You remember when you laid hands on me two nights ago? Well, I have felt even worse since. Indeed I always feel worse after you lay hands on me!' 'Faithful are the wounds of a friend.' That stopped me dead in my tracks and I do

not know that I ever laid hands on anyone else until one night a mature leader deeply used in bringing people to the baptism asked me to lay hands on another. I obeyed and as I prayed I learned an inner secret of the ministry. As I was taken up with God the man on whom I laid hands received power. As I turned from God and became taken up with what was happening to the man, power faded. Quickly I learned and the man was fully baptized. I learned then to move under God and have never forgotten it. Be careful in this realm for the sake of others, and where exorcism is concerned be careful for your own sake as well.

3) *The Place of 'Tongues'.* I found a completion of experience with the loosing of the tongue. The effect of speaking in tongues went far beyond the utterance of the words. Something happened deep down in my inner being. Something critical happened. The part of us which controls language is known by psychologists to be of vital importance. When control of our vocal organs—whether in tongues or in prophecy—passes to God, something of deep significance takes place. Do not downgrade tongues.

4) *Forewarning.* Two rather remarkable things happened just prior to my baptism. It is amazing how God gives forewarning. There came a point when He showed me coming temptation. A whole situation came before me, as in a cameo, while as yet nothing had broken surface. Then there came with the picture a verse of poetry from which He spoke:

> Be firm!
> Whatever tempts thy soul
> To loiter ere it reach its goal
> That thing resist. Go bravely on
> And till the victor's crown be won
> Be firm!

The words went through and through my mind. I recognized the danger when it came and by His mercy did not go down. It ended as I prepared for the baptism.

I have noticed that before an advance in the things of God there is often a time of temptation. If we succumb, the door of opportunity may open and we may recognize it, but we are unable to go through it—we are weak like shorn Samson. On the other hand, if we endure the temptation we are able, in the day of opportunity, to take new ground for God. As one writer said: 'Often when God is about to make princes of us, we make fools of ourselves.' It is so true. Recognize the devices of Satan on this matter. To be forewarned is to be forearmed. There really are spiritual laws which, when obeyed, result in rich fruit. Spiritual things are not vague and chancy but terribly real and often very predictable. As Finney taught: the farmer sows a crop and expects to reap a harvest. It is a natural law. We sow spiritual seed and if we obey spiritual laws the harvest is every bit as sure. Spiritual law is even more certain than natural law.

5) *The Renewal of the Mind.* A second similar, but happier, experience also befell me—this time immediately prior to my baptism. At first I just could not understand it. There came to me that text, 'Lean not upon your own understanding.' It went through and through my mind like a refrain. I knew clearly that God was speaking to me but I did not understand what He was indicating. I felt I was not leaning on my understanding—so why the instruction? I was soon to learn. I was soon to be baptized and find that much of my legalistic background and outlook made things very difficult, e.g. there would be a lady in a house gathering praying without a hat. I was so upset I could hardly pray. I would be in a pentecostal church and the table was not fenced. I was deeply perturbed. I had strong prejudices in many directions. God reminded me of His warning, 'Lean not upon your own understanding,' and I began to find peace. Then one day, one glorious day, He seemed in a wonderful way to wash out and renew my mind. I became a free man in Christ and never again went into a man-made bondage. I must acknowledge too my indebtedness to Nor-

man Grubb, whose writings greatly helped me to this same end.

For the wonderful gifts of salvation and the baptism in the Holy Spirit what can one say? Glory be to God! I greatly rejoice and as the days pass, the joy deepens. The waters are warm. Do come in and be carried along in this glorious River of God. May God bless you.

Note

[1] *Charles G. Finney: An Autobiography* (Fleming H. Revell Company, 1876), p. 20.

12

Questions and Answers

Question:

I do not want to lose my birthright but I am confused about doctrine. I have been taught that I received the Holy Spirit at my conversion. You speak of the baptism as a separate and different experience and I am almost persuaded by the case you have made. My background training, however, has left me with an element of doubt. What should I do?

Answer:

I too was taught in early days exactly as you have been, but I noticed as I pointed out in chapter 11 that men like Charles G. Finney and C. T. Studd had deep experiences in the Holy Spirit after conversion. Studd spoke of 'the baptism of the Spirit' and Finney could write: 'I almost literally bellowed out the unutterable gushings of my heart.' This had a profound effect on me and together with Scripture caused me to seek God very particularly. I prayed the prayer quoted in chapter 11 and God Himself answered me and also cleared my understanding. Be real with God and He will be real with you. Re-read chapters 9 and 11 carefully.

Question:

I believe there is a greater fulness of the Spirit for me than I received at conversion, but I have been taught that I did receive that and now only require to let the experience be outworked. You teach that the baptism is a separate and distinct experience. I am confused. How should I pray? I am particularly anxious not to lose my birthright over an argument about semantics.

Answer:

Were you with me I would say, 'Let us pray together.' You might look for an outworking of an earlier experience. I would be looking for an initial baptism for you. On receiving, you might think it is the former. I would view it as the latter. From one point of view, does it matter? You would reach the same place in the end.

Question:

What about great saints of the past and present who are not pentecostal and have never spoken in tongues, nor prophesied? Were they baptized in the Spirit or not?

Answer:

I am thankful to one of my daughters (who in her university days had her own battle on this front) for shedding light on this problem. One day she pointed out something I had not particularly noticed. Peter, James, John and the apostles had been out with the seventy and had been greatly used of God. They had healed the sick and cast out demons. They knew the Holy Spirit. Christ indeed could say: 'He abideth with you, and shall be in you.' It was these men who were commanded to tarry for the baptism. They too had to go into the upper room. I freely acknowledge that there have been, and are, men of God, used of God, who have not had the baptism; but how much mightier many of them become when they do receive. Sometimes such a one, in the earlier state, is compared with a young and immature pentecostal believer. Do not do this. Rather let a man compare himself not with others but with what he himself may become with the fulness. Apollos was a mighty man before he was more perfectly instructed in the way of the Lord. He may well have outstripped many of the young Christians in many ways—but let us compare him with what he was to become. Spurgeon is often instanced. He was indeed used of God. He brought men to-Christ. So did Peter prior to Pentecost. Peter also healed the sick and cast out demons; yet Peter had to go into the upper room. Do you think that Spurgeon would have been an exception?* Let us base our teaching and practice on the clear word of God.

Question:

I believe I have received the baptism but I have never spoken in tongues or prophesied. You think my experience is incomplete. I am anxious to have my full birthright but am not wholly convinced you are right. What should I do?

Answer:

Friend, if you too were with me, I would say, Scripture explicitly encourages you to desire earnestly spiritual gifts. Tongues and prophecy are spiritual gifts. Come let us pray. You think you have the baptism. I do not think you have. If the power of God comes on you and you speak in tongues, you may think you are receiving a gift. I will see evidence that you are receiving your baptism. We will use different terms—but we will come to the same point in the end.

---

* For evidence that has since come into my hands indicating that Spurgeon spoke in tongues, see Appendix 2.

Question:

Some good men have taught that the baptism is received by faith. They say, 'It is for you. Believe that you have it, and by so doing, it will be yours.' Do you agree?

Answer:

There is a difference between claiming something by faith, and actually receiving it. A person should claim, but he or she should also tarry until that which is claimed is received. Too many have been tricked by substituting the believing for the receiving, and have gone empty away. Long ago Finney pointed out this fallacy in connection with 'the prayer of faith'—showing the danger of a belief that rested upon nothing but itself. An example will simplify the matter. A missionary is engaged upon God's work and is in need of a hundred pounds. He takes this by faith, and in due time God honours this faith and sends the money, enabling him to meet his commitments. Now, until the hundred pounds are received, he remains unable to meet these commitments. His belief pays no bills. There is a difference between believing that the money will come (nay, that in God's purposes it is already as good as his) and his actual, practical receiving of it. So with the baptism. Let it be taken by faith, but do not let the person so doing depart from the condition of tarrying, until he receives in practice. It is obvious that in Acts 2 something other than an inner faith experience took place. Those seeking had faith assuredly—they tarried—but the actual reception of the Spirit was a matter not of faith, but of knowledge and experience.

Question:

In 1 Corinthians 12:13 we read: 'For in one Spirit were we all baptized into one body, whether Jews or Greeks, whether bond or free; and were all made to drink of one Spirit.' Is this not the baptism in the Spirit and is it not necessarily experienced by all Christians?

Answer:

I refer you to chapter 10, where I write of this; but since this point is frequently raised perhaps I should add a little.

Let us consider baptism generally. The Israelites were baptized in the cloud and in the sea unto Moses. John baptized in water unto repentance. Christians are baptized in water into the name of the Father and the Son and the Holy Spirit. Now the Israelites were not baptized in the cloud and in the sea to make them followers of Moses but because they were his followers. Men were not baptized by John to make them repent but because they had repented. Christians are not baptized in water to make them followers of Christ but because they already are His followers. In the same way men are not baptized in the Spirit to make them members of the church, the Body of Christ, but because they are members of that church.

Thus baptism in the Spirit is not an initiation to the Body but is a distinct and different experience from it. Conversion gave entrance there and on the grounds of membership of the church, baptism in the Spirit is given. The position really is quite clear: the Spirit initiates a person, on salvation, into the church which is His Body. The person is at that point baptized into the Body and this happens to all Christians. They are born of the Spirit, sealed with the Spirit and drink of the Spirit. Christ, on the other hand, is the One who initiates a person into the Holy Spirit. He is the Baptizer in the Holy Spirit as John said He would be. The experience is reserved for people who are already in the Body. The two positions should never be confused.

Question:

I would like to be baptized. What should I do?

Answer:

First, be in touch with God. If you find that difficult, search with your Bible to find what hinders. Be prepared to be done with sin. Get a right attitude.

Secondly, read Scripture—particularly Acts 1 and 2 and the other cases where we read of people actually receiving. Note that there is a promise in Acts 2: 'For to you is the promise, and to your children, and to all that are afar off, even as many as the Lord our God shall call unto him.' You are a saved person. You may not have lived in Peter's day, or in the next generation—but the promise is to all who are afar off—even to as many as God would call. This includes you; so, as a person called of God you can claim the promise. This gives a ground for faith and confidence. You will find God will meet this faith and there is no reason why He will not pour out His Spirit on you as on millions of others today if you come in the right way.

You may say, 'I have tried this, and am still not baptized.' I would advise you to continue to seek privately but also to seek help from those who have a ministry in this field. Do remember that while in the New Testament the baptism was spontaneously outpoured on two occasions, on other three occasions it came with the laying on of hands. There are men and women of God who are used in this way in our day. Such a one will probably be able to discern if there is still sin to be dealt with, or areas of difficulty to be resolved. Moreover, in the actual laying on of hands, you may expect the power of God to come on you and the full baptism to be received. The position is very similar to salvation. Many who have difficulty in finding Christ on their own do find Him under the preaching of a man with the gift of evangelism. Similarly many who are not baptized alone do receive very easily when under ministry which God has ordained for this purpose.

Question:

Is there anything special that people used in laying on hands for the baptism practice?

Answer:

Not really. The ministry comes from God. The person laying on hands is like a channel between God and the person seeking. He cannot make it happen but he can be used if God pours out His power. There is no technique. If I am persuaded that a person is prepared and ready I remind him that Christ breathed on the disciples and said, 'Receive ye the Holy Spirit,' and that He still breathes on men today. I remind him that the Holy Spirit glorifies Christ and directs attention to Christ. I ask him to go into Christ—not to take a hopeful leap into the unknown but to go to the Christ he already knows through conversion—to concentrate on Him, indeed to breathe in of Him. In the out-breathing I encourage him to praise the Lord—for which there is scriptural warrant (see Psalm 150). It should be said, however, that people can do all these things and not receive. The real experience comes from God and cannot be man-induced.

Question:

What does the baptism feel like?

Answer:

Wonderful, glorious, unique. You enter another dimension. There is a sense in which you go on to the operating table of

God, and you can trust Him wholly. For some the first impact means repentance and cleansing and this is followed by empowering. It can all happen in one sitting—but the end is always glorious. You are made whole and know it. None whom I have known who has had the experience ever regrets it. None would go back to the pre-baptism position. Do go on into the fulness.

Question:

I have heard of people who have professed to have the baptism going into sin and bringing shame to the name of Christ. How is this?

Answer:

I too have heard of non-pentecostal Christians doing exactly the same thing, and this in no way affects the truth of Christianity. At the time I began to be interested in the baptism I remember criticisms of what had happened in this or that life, in that church, etc. I found this very irrelevant. Mistakes of men in our day in no way affected the teachings of the New Testament on the baptism. If somebody in our day had an unreal experience what was that to me? I wanted an experience such as Paul had and such as he taught. Never stumble over this kind of thing. As long as men are in the body they are prone to sin, and while the baptism gives power to live victoriously, it is still possible for men to make shipwreck if they go temptation's way. The nearer a man gets to God, the greater will be Satan's opposition. Tragedies do occur, and such should result in our prayer for those concerned and not in criticism of their perfectly valid former experiences of God.

My father was a farmer and was a solitary Christian in a country community. He loved Christ and witnessed for Him faithfully. Sometimes he met the criticism, 'Well, if so-and-so is a Christian I don't want anything to do with it.'

He had a memorable way of dealing with this. In the couthy vernacular he would say, 'If you were dry (thirsty— for English friends!) and you wanted a drink and there was an auld deid sheep lyin' in the burn (stream) where would you go for the drink? Above the sheep or below it? 'Above it, of course,' would be the reply. 'Well,' he would say, 'have some sense—go above the life that is polluting the water. Go right up the burn to the fountain-head—right up to Christ Himself. The water is pure up there. Go and drink.' This is worth remembering.

Part Two

Effects of the Baptism

The Testimonies of
Allan Wiggins and James Lunan

Allan Wiggins and James Lunan have both come from one of the most deprived and toughest districts of Greenock. Their testimonies are a tribute to the grace and goodness of God.

13

From the Bottle to the Bible
The Testimony of Allan Wiggins

Allan Wiggins is a young man of thirty-four and is presently in his fourth and final year in the Glasgow Bible College. He is a member of the Assemblies of God in Greenock and vice-president of the local Full Gospel Business Men's Fellowship International (FGBMFI). In a very short period he has become recognized as an evangelist and is in much demand. The results of his ministry are impressive. From the background of his experiences much may be learned of spiritual principle.

I think readers will find much in the following pages of unusual interest, and some of it almost mind-boggling. Another author might have been tempted to leave some of it out—but then I know the man and I also know the devil with whom Allan has had to contend. Above all I know the God who has stood by His child.

While Allan makes only an incidental reference to the occasion, he seems to have had remarkable results in a short visit to the United States last year. He was granted a brief leave of absence from college and preached to about fifty thousand people over about ten meetings. The response was very great. He has arranged to go again in this present session, and we wish him God's rich blessing.

He tells his own story.

Down to the Gutter

I was born in 1960 in the bottom flat of a tenement in Gibshill, Greenock. My mother must have been a very proud lady with delusions of grandeur for this new arrival, for she named me Duncan Allan Kilpatrick Wiggins. Children in Gibshill were usually called Senga, or Wullie. The name had to be shortened and I am now known as Allan.

My mother died in childbirth in August 1963; the child also succumbed. Two days before Christmas of the same year my father died in hospital from cancer in the throat. My parents' death left me and my two brothers facing the daunting prospect of spending our childhood in an orphanage.

My father's sister and her husband, who had a large family of their own, would not let this happen to us, so they became our guardians. (This was a great sacrifice for them.)

Ever since I can remember, my parents' death had a terrible effect on me. I felt as if I was different from all the kids in Gibshill; I resented the fact that they had mums and dads and I didn't. I was an angry young man from a very early age. Yet at night on my own I would cry myself to sleep because my mum and dad were dead.

Growing up in Gibshill was exciting. There was always an abundance of activities in which we waifs and strays could indulge. We played games that children today (including my own) have never heard of: games such as hide and seek, kick the can, peevers, British bulldog, tig, and of course my favourite: Kiss, kick or torture. To the uninitiated, this game was played like tig, only it was girls versus boys. When the girls caught you you had a choice. You could kiss them all, or they could all kick you, or torture you. I accepted torture every time, as a kiss from all those Gibby girls would have turned my hair white before I was ten.

We graduated from such games to more grown-up

activities such as cutting a rope in the back green and tying the rope to all the six doors in a tenement; then we would knock on the doors and watch all the neighbours trying to get their doors open.

Times were hard in the sixties in the Gibby. I was selling the *Evening Times* and *Citizen* outside the pubs in Port Glasgow when I was eight years of age. In these days my uncle was in charge of the paper sellers and on a Saturday evening they would all congregate in 19 Laburnum Street. The Eldorado (fortified wine) would be flowing freely, and we would watch in amazement as all the men would get drunk. They would all sing together, laugh together, cry together, fight each other, and then drop off one by one to sleep as the drink took its toll. This was when my two brothers and I would go into action. We would take the shoes off the sleeping men and search their socks for money that they were stealing from my uncle; for every ten bob note we found we were given half-a-crown's reward from our uncle. We loved the weekends, and I could not wait until I could get involved in all the action I witnessed every week.

In Gibshill we all had nicknames, and I was known locally as 'Wiggy fae ra Gibby'. This nickname has stuck to me all the years. Gibshill was a violent area in the sixties and seventies. In fact gang warfare in Greenock was rife. I couldn't wait to join the Gibby gang because then I would be able to put my violent thoughts into action.

I started getting drunk at thirteen years of age (I had tasted alcohol long before that), and straight away I loved the effect: I loved the excitement, and I loved the immoral lifestyle that came with it.

Looking back, however, I can see God's hand on my life. One incident when I was thirteen comes to mind. We had been drinking the Eldorado on the street corner. A rival gang came and we fought them and beat up some of them pretty badly. We decided to head up to an old railway line at the back of the scheme, where we gathered in a field and proceeded to finish the carry-out. I blacked out and didn't come to until the next morning, when I found myself lying in bed with my doctor standing over me. I was pretty badly cut up. I had been found by a man at the bottom of a gully near that old railway line at three o'clock in the morning. To this day he does not know why he decided to walk the hills at such an hour. I was choking on my vomit and he resuscitated me and carried me home. God's hand was on my life even then.

At sixteen years of age I left Port Glasgow High School and started work as an apprentice with Baird Bros the builders. I was an apprentice bricklayer. I was in a squad of bricklayers who worked hard, drank hard and played hard. They were a tough, uncompromising bunch, and very soon I was one of the boys and partook in all their activities, some legal and others illegal.

At this period in my life I had two loves: the Eldorado and Glasgow Rangers football team. I followed Rangers everywhere they played and actively involved myself in the religious bigotry that goes hand in hand with Rangers and Celtic. I absolutely hated Roman Catholics and was involved in sending money to Northern Ireland to help the Loyalists buy guns to murder the IRA and innocent Catholics.

One day there was an incident not unlike that which befell the evangelist Nicky Cruz, when Dave Wilkerson went to him and told him Jesus loved him. I was standing drinking with the gang at the Gibby shops when three teenagers like myself came to us and started to talk to us about Jesus. A girl in the Christian group turned to me and said, 'Wiggy, Jesus loves you.' She kept on saying this over and over. I told her to shut up or I would slash her face.

She replied, 'Jesus loves you, and I'm not frightened of you. It does not matter how many times you slash me; it will not change the fact that Jesus loves Wiggy from the Gibby.'

She had obviously read *The Cross and the Switchblade*!

I walked away and she called after me again, 'Jesus loves you!'

I could not cope with anyone loving me, let alone Jesus Christ, the Son of God. I could not get this girl out of my head, and no matter how much wine I drank I still heard in my head her words, 'Jesus loves you.'

I started to go out with a girl of my own age called Kathleen, who had been brought up beside me. Both families warned her not to have anything at all to do with me as I would bring her nothing but trouble. They were quite correct in their assessment of the situation. Our three-year courtship was stormy to say the least. I treated Kathleen very badly in those years and indeed in the years of marriage that followed.

Even though I was constantly drinking and getting into trouble, there was always a yearning within me to better myself. I decided to study hard at building college and in my last year as an apprentice, to the surprise of many, I gained the Silver Trowel Award (there were only six in Britain awarded that year). As a result of this advanced craft award, I very soon became a bricklaying instructor. I taught apprentices brickwork theory during the day and at night I got stuck into the drink and the nonsense that goes with it.

At twenty years of age Kathleen and I were married in Greenock Registry Office. I would not get married in a church because by this time I was an atheist. My wedding night was a fiasco. I was carried into bed at 8:30 p.m. in the evening, unconscious with the drink. This was the beginning of our married life together.

Four years after we were married our first child, Alicia, was born. This should have been a very joyful occasion for both of us, but sadly for me it was just another excuse for the drink.

Sobriety

Six months after Alicia's birth I found myself in Ravenscraig Hospital. At twenty-four years old, married with a child, here I was in Ravenscraig out of my mind with drink. During my hospital stay, a fellow patient suggested that I try Alcoholics Anonymous. We were duly given permission to attend the Saturday evening meeting of AA which met in the Red Cross rooms in West Blackhall Street, Greenock. Four of us set out to that meeting. Two of them are now dead (from drink-related causes), and the third is in Erskine Hospital with a 'wet brain'.

The speaker gave his testimony, and to be truthful I heard very little of it. But one thing he said struck a chord:

'If you don't pick up the first drink it is impossible to get drunk.'

I wondered why I had never thought of that years earlier; I would not have been in such a mess later.

I attended AA regularly and on my release from hospital I went back to Kathleen and Alicia. Eight months into my sobriety I was given my old job back and life was getting better.

Alcoholics Anonymous teaches that alcoholism is a three-fold illness: physical, mental and spiritual, and it has a Twelve Step programme which helps with the so-called spiritual side of the illness. It was suggested that because of my attitude I should look at this programme. The first step involved our admission that 'we were powerless over alcohol' and 'that our lives had become unmanageable'. I had no problem with this; my life was totally unmanageable due to my dependence on alcohol.

The second step encouraged us 'to believe that a Power greater than ourselves could restore us to sanity'. I had no problems with the second part of this step; I knew I needed restored to sanity. However, I could not believe for a moment that there was a power greater than myself.

The third step upset me so much that I decided they

could keep their steps. This one instructed us to make 'a decision to turn our wills and our lives over to the care of God *as we understood Him*'.

I decided that I would ask all those AA members who spoke of 'God *as [they] understood Him*' to explain to me what they understood about God. The sad thing is that out of the many members I spoke to only one (a lady from Paisley) could explain to me anything about this God.

She said, 'God as I understand Him is the Father of the Lord Jesus Christ, and the only way to Him is by His Son Jesus.'

I didn't want to hear this. Her next statement almost gave me a heart attack.

'Also this God of my understanding, the Lord Jesus Christ, loves you.'

I immediately recalled that crazy Christian girl in Gibshill who had told me the same.

After two years of sobriety our second child, Diane, was born. My wife commanded me to go and see the local minister so that Diane could be christened. He agreed to do this two days before Christmas. During the service (as I know now, but did not know then) I came under conviction. I knew I was living a double life. The only thing that had changed was that I was no longer getting drunk. This saddens me greatly. Had I not found Christ I could have stayed in AA until my dying days, stayed sober, and yet ended up in hell for all eternity. This vague 'higher power' concept that so many AA members speak of is blinding them to the fact that eternal life can only be found through a personal relationship with the Lord Jesus Christ. Praying merely to a higher power will only bring hell for all eternity. It is only Jesus who sets people free.

Conversion

On Christmas Day 1986 I declared to my wife Kathleen that I was going to the kirk to find God. My poor wife thought that I was having a relapse and would be back in Ravenscraig pretty soon.

Putting on my best suit I headed for the kirk, deciding that if there was a God then surely He would speak to me on Christmas Day. The first thing I noticed on entering the church was just how miserable all the congregation looked. You would have thought that on at least that one day of the year they would be happy.

I walked right down to the very front pew in the church and sat down. Looking around me, I knew that some of the people were speaking about me. An old lady appeared beside me. She owned one of the loudest voices I have ever had the displeasure of hearing.

She said, 'EXCUSE ME, YOUNG MAN, THAT'S MY SEAT!'

I knew nothing about sanctification in those days. I replied, 'Has it got your name written on it?'

She said, 'Yes!' And sure enough, on the door of the pew was her family name.

I got up to leave the church, but recognizing one of the local criminal fraternity I sat beside him and got through the remainder of the service. I did not hear from God that Christmas Day. However, every Sunday after Christmas I went back to that same church.

After a Sunday morning service in February 1987, the minister gave me a copy of the Good News version of the gospel of Luke. He requested that I read the first chapter before attending the communicants' class on the Monday.

I started to read the gospel. Before I knew where I was, I was reading the tenth chapter, and on I continued. In reading I came to realize that this Jesus was a good man: He was speaking to and helping the dregs of His society. I noticed that Jesus was speaking to people that would be turned away from many churches today. I quite liked this Jesus Christ of Nazareth, and I hated the Pharisees who I knew were trying to set Jesus up.

When I reached the twenty-third chapter I was totally

engrossed in the proceedings. This chapter brought me to my knees. Reading of the two criminals crucified with Jesus, I was astounded that one of them started to call Jesus names and then he said, 'If you are the Christ, save yourself and us' (v. 39). I thought to myself of many a time in my life when I had called God names.

The second criminal rebuked the first and replied: 'This *man* (Jesus) has done nothing wrong' (v. 41).

Then in the very next breath, his dying breath, he uttered those most remarkable words: '*Lord*, will you remember me when you come into your kingdom?' (v. 42). In a split second of time this thief had a revelation from God that took him from 'man' to 'Lord' (vv. 41–2).

Jesus replied, 'Assuredly I say to you, today you shall be with me in Paradise' (v. 43).

Salvation had come to a dying thief. He was plucked from the very gates of hell and brought forth into the glorious kingdom of the living God. In an instant he was brought from darkness into light.

I could not contain myself any longer. I burst into tears. Big, hard 'Wiggy fae ra Gibby' was crying his eyes out. I realized that Jesus was not just a good man, but that He was and is the Son of the Most High God. I was on my knees, and until the day I see my Saviour face to face I shall never forget my prayer:

> God, if You are real I would ask that You give me the same opportunity as that dying thief. For years I was like the other thief, cursing You and calling You names. Jesus, please come and change me and make me right with God.

There and then I was soundly converted.

Backsliding

Around this time I moved into the insurance industry, and I learned very quickly how to make a lot of money. And this was to lead to a mighty fall.

We moved out of Gibshill to a bought house, and very quickly money became my god. The insurance industry can be an absolute cesspit for Christians. There are many temptations that would pull a man deep into the pit.

A dear Christian lady came to my house and told me, 'If you do not stop putting money and AA before God, God will take everything from you.' (I had become very prominent in AA circles.) She told me that Jesus always had to be given first place in my life, and that God would put me in my place, because I had got too big for my boots. She is a real gentle-spirited lady, and it hurt her very much to deliver this message to me.

Although I had been saved for a year, there was not much fruit in my life. After four years of sobriety I was about to be faced with a very stressful situation. The woman I knew as my mother was given a few weeks to live. I could not cope with this. She died, and at her funeral I knew that I had not fulfilled my duty to Christ. I had failed to proclaim the good news to my own kith and kin. The devil capitalized on this sorrowful condition I found myself in. He came very near, encouraging me to take a little drink. This would console me—one drink wouldn't cause me any harm—no-one would know—I could keep it a secret. 'One drink will help you get a good night's sleep and when you awaken in the morning you'll be all right.' The devil is a liar and I swallowed the lie hook, line and sinker.

I got drunk and caused all sorts of problems. Sin always promises more than it produces. The devil promised me a restful night, but that is not what happened. There is no rest for the wicked. Sin begets more sin. With the drinking came the cheating and the lying.

In an eighteen-month period of backsliding I lost my wife, my two lovely children, my job with the Prudential, my house in Gateside Grove, my car, and more importantly I lost my sanity—all because I listened to a lie of the devil and decided to pursue the way of the flesh.

During those eighteen months I found myself thirteen times in the local psychiatric hospital, locked up for the safety of myself and the public. Each time I was released from the hospital I would go back to church (a pentecostal one by then), but within days I would be drinking again. With the drink came those awful fits of delirium tremens. I would see and come under attack from the most hideous creatures that one could imagine. My wife, who was not a Christian at this point, started divorce proceedings. The hatred for her and my children that this caused was terrible. The devil had me so bound that I hated my own family. I walked past my children in the street as if they did not exist. I was staying in various drinking houses in the Gibby and was deep in sin.

Two people in particular were given burdens to pray for and go after me. There was Jean, the lady who delivered the 'Put God first' message. The other was David, a man with whom I had been in school and whom I later encountered in the Prudential. He and his wife moved from Kilmacolm and bought a house right next to Gibshill; why he did not know.

The Lord placed David Connell right next to me. Thirteen times this family took me in, cleaned me up and took me to the hospital. David was there along with Jean when everyone else had given up hope. Jean visited me in hospital and told me that God had a plan and a purpose for my life, and that He wanted me to go into the ministry. Thirteen times this lady delivered this message. Truly a lady of faith!

I left the hospital for my thirteenth and final time and went to a rehabilitation centre in Kilmacolm. The Haven was largely funded by two relations of Mr Black, Roy Lees and Bill Kerr. I was in quite a depressed state at this time. My divorce was imminent. The times in the psychiatric units had taken their toll. I felt as if I would never be free of this dependence on alcohol. I was a hopeless case. However, little did I know that the fulness of Christ was awaiting Allan Wiggins.

Baptism in the Spirit

I was attending Ken Kyle's church in Kilmacolm, and Ken suggested that we at The Haven should go to Struthers Memorial Church on Saturday evenings. We would be most welcome, and the teaching would help us.

Two days after Ken suggested this we saw an advert in the *Greenock Telegraph* for a Struthers outreach in James Watt College on the Thursday evening. We all attended this meeting and listened to what Miss Mary Black had to say. The following Thursday saw another Struthers outreach at the same venue. We attended this too and I was very impressed by Ruth Gollan's testimony. She spoke of being endued with power to be a witness for Christ in this generation. This power to be a witness struck a chord within me. Mr Black then preached from Mark's Gospel. Then, as he always does, he made a no nonsense, no fancy frills, altar call. I knew that this might be my last opportunity to get right with God. My thoughts were: 'I am not good enough to receive the baptism in the Spirit; I'm a no-hoper.'

Mr Black at this point came and asked where we were from.

We replied, 'The Haven in Kilmacolm.'

He said, 'That's interesting. I used to feed pigs there!' And nothing had changed—we were a sorry-looking sight!

Mr Black and Miss Jennifer Jack prayed with me for the baptism and within minutes I was baptized in the Spirit. God's goodness did not end there, because there was deep deliverance which was way beyond me. I was endued with the power from on high. From that evening I have never stopped being a witness for Christ.

I went to see my wife and children on the Sunday. The divorce was only a matter of weeks away. My wife Kathleen on meeting me *saw* the change in my life. She *saw* that something had happened to me. Just before returning to The Haven that evening I gave my wife a letter about forgiveness. That very evening she got down on her knees before God and asked Him to give to her what He had given to me. She asked Christ into her life that evening. And she went to her solicitor and cancelled the divorce the following day. Within one week we were reconciled with each other and with Almighty God.

Preparation for Service

While at The Haven I found myself writing out sermons. This continued when I went home. I did not know why I was doing this. I put it down to the fact that the Bible had taken on a whole new meaning when I was baptized in the Spirit.

I spent every day in Struthers' Coffee Shop speaking with and learning from Mr Black. I had realized very early on in attending the Saturday evening meetings that this man lived close to God and knew the deep things of God. I studied Mr Black's sermons with great gusto and I tried to carry out the practical applications that he brings into every sermon.

I was and still am learning to listen to God. Feeling in my spirit that God was calling me to Bible college, I sought counsel of Mr Black, who suggested that it would be a good idea to go ahead.

At this time I had been invited to a number of churches to preach or to give my testimony. This is why I had spent so much time studying and writing sermons from God's word. I had never thought for a moment that I would become a preacher, far less an evangelist.

I was accepted for Glasgow Bible College and duly went there. Before long more doors were opening for me. I was allowed to preach in churches to which I would never have been asked had I not been at the College.

In my first year fellow-students would say to me that I would make a good pastor or assistant-pastor. I very nearly went along with their ideas about my calling, and if I had I would have missed the harvest. I would never make a good pastor; it is not my calling. I am an evangelist.

Someone asked me very recently: 'How do you know that you are an evangelist?'

My answer was simple and to the point: 'I know because I see people getting saved, healed, delivered and baptized in the Spirit everywhere I go.' Power evangelism is the only way forward for the church in these last days. If you are not prepared to demonstrate the kingdom of God after you have proclaimed the good news, then you might be as well keeping your mouth closed. There are far too many talkers in the Kingdom, not enough demonstrators. The gospel is and always has been a power encounter. The demonstration in signs and wonders bursts the very gates of hell. Praise God!

Almighty God brings our ministries deeper and deeper on a gradual basis, and I thank God for this. If at first He had bestowed on me the power evangelism concept that I know now, it would have destroyed me. An evangelist, Mervyn Milne from Perth, said as much to me in a word of knowledge. He was quite correct.

At the end of my first year in Bible college, things were going pretty well. Everywhere I went to preach, signs and wonders followed. Many people were converted, healed and baptized in the Spirit throughout different denominations.

Watch Out for the Devil

Coming to the end of the first college year, the devil had a go at me, and I succumbed to temptation. I found myself in a deep, deep pit of sin which lasted for six days and six nights. I received a glimpse of the enemy and of a state that I did not realize existed. He gained a foothold in my life and almost killed me; this is not an exaggeration. I found myself in Inverclyde Royal Hospital lapsing in and out of consciousness. People were coming to see me, and I cannot now remember their being there.

I was physically, mentally and spiritually bankrupt.

There was absolutely no fight within me. This was the same man who only weeks earlier, whilst preaching in Glasgow, had witnessed sixty-three people getting saved. I was reduced to a helpless, hopeless wreck.

My best friend Terry came to see me in hospital. An unforgettable recollection of his visit is the shock on his face as he saw how sick I was. Terry, on leaving the hospital, went immediately to Mr Black and told him that 'the bishop' was in trouble. ('The bishop' is Mr Black's pet name for me.) Mr Black already knew this. He was deeply troubled in his spirit and he did something which is evidently quite unusual for him. He sat down and wrote a letter which he delivered personally to me that very day at Inverclyde Royal Hospital. He prayed with me and read the letter out to me; I was too ill to read it for myself. I would like to include this very personal letter in this testimony; its significance is paramount. This is the letter in full.

Dear Allan,
  You have been very much on my mind and spirit over the last week, and I feel I should write to you.
  Watch out for the devil. After a fall when God would gladly raise and restore you the devil will discourage and tell you it's no good, you'll never make it. He is a liar & has been a liar since before the world began. Resist him and he'll flee from you.
  There is nothing you have done which can't be repaired. My heart is full of love for you & the sure knowledge of a way back & not to shame—but to rejoicing in the power of Christ—so you let Him down—did Peter not do that very thing & after knowing Him so deeply. Was he cast off by Christ? Never! He was *fully* restored & given high commission. So will you be. You have a high destiny which by God's grace you will fulfil.
  There is a need however. Just as that night in James Watt College God moved mightily—so will He do again I believe, if you will let Him. Come and see me. There is need for deliverance at a level beyond yourself—but you can be gloriously free—& that permanently.

In our midst you will receive love and never, I believe, a breath of criticism. Do come and see me.

Yours ever in Christ,
H. B. Black
As a father to a beloved son

I believe that this letter was written prophetically. Mr Black just before leaving the hospital warned me that an attack from the devil was imminent. One week later the attack came and I was astounded by its severity. I will describe this attack as it happened, and I would like to make it clear at this stage: never underestimate the devil. This is not an over-dramatized work of fiction. What you are about to read is factual.

I was awakened in my room at 5:30 a.m. The sun was streaming through the curtains. However, there was a darkness in the room which was unbearable. The enemy came and told me that I was finished, I would never preach again, I would never see anyone saved or healed or baptized in the Spirit, I would never get back to Bible college. He told me that my ministry as an evangelist was over. This hurt me deeply. When you have had a burden for the lost burning away within you every day, to be told this is now over is terrible.

The powers of darkness had now enveloped the room. I started to pray that God would intervene in this situation. I shouted out aloud verses of Scripture and commanded the enemy to leave me in the name of Jesus. The enemy did not leave. He laughed at me. We cannot use Jesus' name like some magic formula: it is just not on. At this stage I was picked up by an unseen supernatural presence and was thrown the full length of the room. To say that I was terrified is an understatement. I picked myself up and had barely got on my feet when I was thrown down again. This time I was almost choked to death. I was praying and crying, but the enemy's attack went on relentlessly. I tried to read my Bible, but I couldn't. I was dragged backwards across the room away from my Bible. The violence of this assault lasted about five minutes; the whole experience took almost three hours.

I suddenly realized that Mr Black's letter was on my table. I moved to get the letter, and all hell broke loose. I was thrown bodily again across the room. I eventually got to the letter and opened it, crying out to God to help me. I started to read the letter: '[The devil is] a liar.... Resist him...God [will] gladly restore you...You have a mighty destiny.' The glory of God filled the room, Christ the deliverer came, and the powers of darkness were smashed just as they were at the cross two thousand years earlier. Christ came and filled me with His love. A couple of days later I went to Mr Black for ministry and explained to him that I believed that his letter was prophetic. Everything that it mentioned came to pass.

Mr Black gave me good news that day. He said, 'Now that you have met the devil face to face, you will be glad to know that God will use you in deliverance.' He was proved to be quite correct. Deliverance became a dimension of my ministry that at first I felt I could well have done without.

Restoration

Almighty God restored me. I went back to College, and before long I was back preaching again. Praise God! At about this time I became involved with the FGBMFI, and I recognized pretty quickly that the Lord Christ would move in power in these meetings. One facet I have recognized about deliverance ministry is this: if your life is not pure and honouring to God, please do not pray with anyone for deliverance. The devil would have you for breakfast.

I realize that the nearer I draw to God the more aware I become of the movements of the enemy. The attacks that he has launched on my family over the years have been horrendous—but God has always stood by us.

As an evangelist I preach in many different churches and denominations, and the attacks that can come from men of the cloth are unbelievable. On one occasion I was invited to speak in a church in Glasgow. I was to take the whole service, which lasted for an hour (it takes me an hour to warm up). On arrival at the church, the minister met me in the vestry to give me a pep talk. He told me that he would be disappointed if the meeting was not finished by twelve o'clock—he did not say noon or midnight!

He told me that I would preach for eighteen minutes. I would not be allowed to preach the doctrine of hell, or the baptism of the Spirit, and there would most definitely be no altar call. Who needs the devil on your back when you have the devil using a man in a dog collar? The time came for 'the bishop' to deliver the sermon. I looked the minister straight in the eye and said, 'The reading this morning is from Luke's gospel 16:19–31—the rich man in hell.' His face was like thunder, and I thought, 'This man might end up in hell before this sermon is over.' I preached very simply for those eighteen minutes. My points were clear: 'Two men; two ways; two destinies, heaven or hell. It's make-your-mind-up time.' I gave the altar call with Peter's words ringing in my ears: 'We ought to obey God, rather than man!' Words that Mr Black had spoken to me very early in my ministry echoed in my head: 'When Almighty God gives you a message, you be sure and preach it'— words of wisdom indeed from a spiritual father to his young sparrowhawk! Seven people came forward for salvation including an elder with twenty-five years' service in that denomination. (I don't know if he managed to get twenty-six years' service. He was baptized in the Spirit two weeks after salvation.) Thanks be to Almighty God that I obeyed Him and not that poor lost minister.

While on the subject of hell I should say this. I will never apologize for preaching this awful doctrine. I don't care one iota how many people it upsets, for (as the Bible teaches clearly) hell is a real place and people who reject the message of the cross are going there for *all* eternity.

There are too many people listening to academic theologians (many of whom incidentally have hardly witnessed a soul being saved in their man-appointed ministries) disputing if hell is real, if it is for eternity, if it is a purifying place, if unbelievers will go there until they are pure enough for heaven—or will a lost soul be annihilated?

What a load of rubbish! Who in their right mind could believe such drivel? Don't they realize that in disputing hell they are in fact calling the Lord Christ a liar? Almost everything we know about hell was spoken by Him. These theologians (I use this word very loosely) need dangled over hell for a few minutes. They would soon change their tune. Hell is real; it is the price that is paid for rejecting Jesus.

Power Evangelism

Power evangelism is a term that John Wimber coined, and in my view it is the *only* way forward in these last hours. Wimber writes:

> I define power evangelism as a *presentation of the gospel that is rational but also transcends the rational.* The explanation of the kingdom of God comes with a demonstration of God's power through works of power. It is a spontaneous, Spirit-inspired, empowered presentation of the gospel. It is usually preceded and undergirded by demonstrations of God's presence, and frequently results in groups of people being saved. Signs and wonders do not save; *only Jesus saves.*[1]

Jesus proclaimed and demonstrated the gospel wherever He went, and so must we. It is our commission. Proclamation and demonstration go hand in hand and must never be separated. When a denomination or a movement catches the vision of power evangelism, the supernatural becomes the norm. People get saved, healed, baptized in the Spirit, demons are cast out and hell's very gates get pushed back.

I have written seminar material on this subject at the request of a church in America to which I hope to go shortly. However, it is not just for America. In September

1994 I was invited to speak at the Greenock Elim Youth Conference. David Hogg, the youth leader (a man who so much wants the deep things of God), requested that I speak on proclamation and demonstration. These youngsters in attendance caught a glimpse of the kingdom of God that morning and a hunger was instilled in their hearts for the deep things of God. Needs were met in abundance. One girl in particular stays in my memory. She was in a Brethren assembly (there were different denominations at this weekend, praise God). She came forward very tentatively for prayer, explaining that God had spoken to her about going into full-time service for Him, and she was about to give up her job to fulfil this. She said, 'My church does not believe in signs and wonders, but I have *seen* with my own eyes God demonstrate His kingdom here. Please pray that He would demonstrate His power in my life.' Please take note of her words: *I have seen*. This is the testimony of the church right through the book of Acts. People saw and heard. God met her in a mighty way, and that evening she was baptized in the Spirit.

As a roving evangelist preaching throughout denominations my dependence is totally on God for power evangelism. Wimber is one hundred per cent correct in his definition. When the gospel is proclaimed in this way groups of people are set free. I have witnessed this in my short time as an evangelist. I have had the privilege of leading thousands to Christ. This is a fact. I have witnessed large numbers of healings, miracles, signs and wonders. Praise God for every soul that gets saved, virtually every day in life.

I believe that in these last days some of the most dynamic power evangelism battles come over deliverance. There is a mighty move of God in this realm. This, I believe, is power evangelism at its pinnacle.[2]

Battle with Hell

Mr Black has requested that I write about an encounter with the powers of darkness which took place recently. I don't speak too often about deliverance because I am very careful not to underestimate the enemy. This incident of which he wanted me to speak happened in America; for reasons which will become obvious I cannot be more specific, as confidentiality must never be broken.

A lady came forward at an altar call. Now to make you fully aware of the situation, there were approximately two thousand people standing forward for ministry. I was on my own, trying to minister to these people. She said, 'I have a demon. Cast it out of me.'

I told her to sit down as I was not casting out any demons in public. She came again and again with the same request. I gave her the same answer.

The head elder of the church spoke to me a few days later and told me that this lady was requesting deliverance. He said that we should see her as she was probably the main benefactor to the church.* We met with the lady and she was very nice and polite; then all of a sudden she said to the elder, 'You don't believe that I have a demon. Your theology doesn't permit you to believe this.' Then all of a sudden she put her legs up round her neck and her face took on the appearance of a cat (Mr Black calls this a feline spirit). I wasn't quite sure if I should pray or give her a saucer of milk. I had never witnessed anything like this. I was terrified.

This demon became very violent, especially towards the elder. It was playing a game with him, taunting him. At this period I had not said a word, and it felt as if the demon did not recognize that I was there. The elder got pretty upset with the demon, and as a result of this the lady attacked

---

* A very bad reason.—HBB.

him. She tore at his clothes screaming, 'I kill you, I kill you!' I then took action. I hit her over the head with my hardback NIV Bible and prayed very fearfully in tongues. She quietened down for a period; then again she attacked the elder. The demon was calling him all sorts of filthy names that are unprintable. She then switched her attack to me. She tried to hit me, but she could not do this. On two occasions she stopped short about eighteen inches from my face. She could not penetrate the hedge of God.

She then spoke to the elder in response to his screaming at her that he was going to cast the demons out of her. She said, 'You cannot cast anything out of me! You have no authority, your Christian life is a scam! You are a man of unclean lips. You are an adulterer—you are having sex with another man's wife. (She went on to speak of perverse sex acts that they were allegedly engaging in.) I thought at this moment that the elder would be carted off to the asylum.

I spoke out against the demon and told it to stop lying. It repeated its previous statement that the man was in adultery. I spoke to the demon saying that I would cast it out in the Name of Jesus Christ of Nazareth. The demon accused me of being an alcoholic—to which I replied that I had been but was no longer.

What happened next was absolutely mindblowing. The demon said to me: 'Do you forget what happened to you in your room in Greenock?' It then proceeded to relate the incident of a few years earlier and began to taunt me: 'We pulled you all over the floor, we threw you all round the room! You'll never cast us out—you're a nobody!'

I had never been so frightened in all my life. I cried out to God in my spirit. 'Lord, what will I do here?' The revelation came. 'The letter,' I thought, 'Mr Black's letter.'

I said to the devil, 'Yes, that's what happened in that room. However, you have conveniently left out a very important factor: Mr Hugh Black's letter.'

At the very mention of this letter there was a stirring up

of the bowels of very hell itself—intense spiritual demonic attack. A table was overturned, cups thrown over, the lady was thrown across the floor. Hell's pit was spewing out its filth. I pressed on in. I said, 'I have this very letter here in my Bible,' and I started to read it aloud: 'The devil's a liar. Resist him and he will flee from you... God will gladly raise and restore you...you can be gloriously set free.' Praise God, this lady was gloriously set free in an instant. The feline spirit was cast out along with a number of others. There had been much uncleanness in this lady's life in the past, and this is probably where the demons gained a foothold. In her life today she is searching for the deep things of God, and by all accounts she is doing very well indeed.

I was still faced with a dilemma. I would now need to speak with the elder. When I asked him if he was in adultery, he admitted it. He was prayed with and action was taken to deal with the whole sorry situation.

Again I repeat: keep away from deliverance if your life is not pleasing to God. This elder could have been completely destroyed by the power that the enemy had in his life. This encounter was indeed power evangelism in operation.

Future Prospects

I will be returning to America (DV) with my wife and children on a few occasions in the next year. God has opened a door for us in the USA that no man can close. It is a privilege for me to proclaim and demonstrate His glorious gospel. My favourite scripture verse is Hebrews 13:8: 'Jesus Christ is the same, yesterday, today, and forever.' This same Jesus is saving more people today than when He first walked the earth, He is healing more, delivering more, and baptizing in the Spirit vast multitudes. Praise His Name. Salvation, healing and deliverance did not end with the death of the apostles. The Great Commission was given to all believers.

> And these signs will follow those who believe: in my name
> they will cast out demons, they will speak with new tongues.
> They will take up serpents and if they drink anything deadly
> it will by no means hurt them: they will lay hands on the
> sick and they will recover (Mk 16:17–18 NKJV).

What a glorious, victorious commission for all who believe!

It has been a great privilege to write for this book. To be
associated with a book which speaks powerfully and so very
clearly on the baptism in the Spirit is indeed a pleasure. Mr
Black's books throughout the years have been instrumental
in setting many prisoners free. I include myself in this
category. It has been a privilege for me to have sat at this
man's feet over the years drinking in the deep spiritual
things of God that he so ably proclaims. Hugh Black's
influence on my own ministry has been paramount. The
advice and indeed the 'kicks' helped mould, shape and
prepare me for the high calling that God has given me, that
of an evangelist. His servant has truly trained me and
continues to train me in learning to listen to God. I will
always be grateful to him for his never-ending love for me.

As he wrote in his letter, 'As a father to a beloved son', so
I say to him, 'As a son to a beloved father—thank you for
standing on God's glorious word and never compromising.'

Mr Black said to me very recently, 'Who would have
given tuppence for your chances, the night you came for
your baptism? Who would have thought for a moment that
you would be used to bring in a harvest of souls?' Mr Black
recognized God's calling in my life very early on and has
stood faithfully in the gap for me. He even came to my door
one evening very recently and told me that the devil was
after me. He was correct. He stayed, had a cup of tea, ate all
my KitKats, then prayed with me. The devil had again
been put to flight by the man of God in obedience to his
Lord and his Saviour. To God be the glory for ever.

Notes

[1] John Wimber, 'Power Evangelism: Definitions and Directions', in Peter Wagner and F. Douglas Pennoyer, eds., *Wrestling with Dark Angels* (Monarch, 1990), p. 36.

[2] Deliverance out of the bondage of the devil is wonderful, but there is another side to the picture. Sometimes the fulness of glory a soul can go into in Christ is overlooked. There is indeed a ministry which a few receive to help others to enter this dimension. In my view it is one of the most important ministries there is. For fuller treatment of this subject see Hugh B. Black, comp., *E. H. Taylor: A Modern Christian Mystic* (New Dawn Books, 1994). This may be power ministry at an even higher level than the one Allan indicates.—HBB.

14

From Gangland to Glory Land
The Testimony of Jimmy Lunan

Jimmy Lunan has already figured in one of my earlier books, *Christ the Deliverer*, where the story of his remarkable healing from rheumatoid arthritis is included. But there are other areas in Jimmy's life and experience which are of unusual interest, and some of these are told in this present book—in particular, the violent background of his early days, his conversion, his baptism in the Spirit, a second phenomenal healing and his experience of deliverance. To keep a unity in the narrative, his first healing and the visitation of angels, first recorded in *Christ the Deliverer*, are included here. Jimmy's experience is indeed a testimony to both the love and the power of God, and is a very suitable record to include under the general title of this book: *The Baptism of the Spirit and Its Effects*.

In the previous testimony Allan told his own story. In Jimmy's case it has been written from material supplied by him and his wife Maureen.

Early Violence

Jimmy was fourth in a family of six and is now thirty-nine years of age. He was born in Chalmers Street, Greenock, on the border of the Gibshill area, and later moved to Poplar Street, right in the heart of the scheme.

Jimmy's family were not without a form of religion. They were deeply involved in the Orange Order, but very early the boy realized that while the Order had the trappings of religion it was not necessarily Christian. He did not of course define the matter in these terms then, but he intuitively sensed hypocrisy. At first he was pleased with the uniforms and the marching, and he joined in the hatred of Catholics. Despite the façade, however, all was not well at home. There were bad fights in the family, largely through his father's drunkenness.

Jimmy himself first became involved in serious violence at the age of six when he attacked a boy of about ten or eleven with a bottle. To this day he remembers the blood. Jimmy's mother attended to the other boy. Until this incident Jimmy had been very close to his mother—but this caused a breach. A deep bond was damaged and indeed has never been fully restored. He had seen the violence of his father to his mother before this point and had hated it. But something changed when he himself became violent. It seemed that an evil spirit entered him. Indeed in later years when he experienced deliverance God brought him back in spirit to this early incident.

Schools and Borstals

Violence continued. Jimmy formed a young gang and they began to beat up pupils from St Mungo's (a Catholic primary school) very severely. He went to primary school himself in Ladyburn, and his education there seems to have been little short of a fiasco. He describes his attitude as rebellious - and, when he went into secondary school, as totally rebellious. Even in his primary days he found himself in court for stealing and other misdemeanours.

Jimmy's behaviour in secondary school almost beggars belief. At that time in Scotland discipline was generally very good and the school he attended was not a soft option. Staff were well qualified, capable and conscientious—but Jimmy was in a class by himself. That, I fear, is an unfortunate phrase—for the fact is that generally he wasn't in a class at all. His behaviour was so bad that teachers just couldn't have him in their rooms and he was allowed more or less to wander the school. On one such occasion as he passed a door he saw one of his pals being punished by a master. Jimmy burst in, attacked the teacher with a chair, and threw the belt (used in Scotland instead of the cane) along with the teacher's coat out of the window. On another occasion he ripped a teacher's tyres and smashed her car.

It was at this time that Jimmy moved into the heart of Gibshill, and he found that he had to break his way into a gang there. That meant fighting his way in. This he successfully did. Indeed he formed his own new gang—the Tiny Gibbies. He was about fourteen at the time. There were other two older gangs in the area. The three acted independently but came together against outsider opposition. By this time Jimmy's hostility to Catholics began to cool down. As so often happens in such cases the criminals of both fraternities tend to come together. Religious bigotry becomes less important than the common involvement in crime. Hatred did, however, continue, but aimed now at ethnic minorities and the 'English'. Both were attacked and literally driven out of the area. At this time the gang indulged in shop breaking and protection rackets. There were three ice-cream vans which operated in the area, and Jimmy's gang took money from all three. The fact that protection money was paid did not prevent Jimmy and his friends on one occasion from attacking and robbing one of the vans! Jimmy himself was greatly feared. He terrified shopkeepers, who at times would give him what he wanted for nothing.

With a pal at the age of fifteen he found himself again in court and proved so unruly that he was kept in custody—which was most unusual for his age. He was shipped to a remand centre where he continued to be so disorderly that for a time he was locked up with no clothes. He was in this

institution for two or three months and went in black shorts
with bare feet, whereas other inmates had green uniforms
and shoes. This was to prevent Jimmy from absconding. He
was allowed to play football (theoretically) but since the
pitch was a gravel one and he had bare feet it was impossible. He managed to acquire keys for every room in the
place, but for much of his time he was locked in the 'cooler'.

From the remand home he was sent back to Greenock
Juvenile Court, which sentenced him to a term in an
approved school. But while locked in a cell waiting to go to
Kibble, Jimmy, with four or five others (also destined for
various approved schools), broke out. He was soon caught
and found himself at Kibble. He seems to have approved of
the discipline there. But he was allowed to go home at
weekends and at home his law-breaking continued. Until
he was old enough to go to jail Jimmy was in five institutions: Bellfield, Kibble, Longriggend, Barlinnie and
Glenochil. For two and a half years he was in approved
schools, and he spent his fifteenth, sixteenth, seventeenth
and eighteenth birthdays in close confinement.

Deepening Violence

The next part of this narrative makes horrendous reading,
and I should point out that Jimmy has been most reticent
about his life of violence. Never once since his conversion
has he told details in public—or to me in private either. I
knew the background was there, and it was only as I probed
that he revealed it. He takes no pride in it at all. But I feel
that the depths of his sin throws into sharp relief the power
of God in his redemption. The extent of the change is quite
phenomenal. From a man of extreme violence Jimmy has
become a man of great kindness and indeed gentleness.

The story, I feel, must be told—but it is not for the faint-
hearted. The account is in no way full, but I have selected
enough incidents to give a true picture of the state of affairs.

Battle with the Police

On a weekend at home he robbed an ice-cream van and had a running battle with a policeman. One night he broke into an electricity substation and blacked out the whole area. He then attacked the same policeman, hitting him on the head with a wine bottle. Two policemen grabbed his pal and handcuffed him between them. Jimmy with six or seven others then attacked them and stole their walkie-talkies and hats. They would be in difficulties because of the handcuffing. Reinforcements, however, arrived and took their pal away. The gang escaped.

Press-ganging the Cows

The next incident, while serious, is amusing. A brewer's lorry tipped off six barrels of beer at a social club and Jimmy planned to steal the whole consignment, but he was faced with a major problem. The barrels were too heavy for him to carry and they were too heavy for his older brother too, who was stronger than Jimmy. But our friend was a young man of unusual initiative. I can hardly believe the plan he evolved. He went up the hill behind Gibshill and abducted three cows. These he drove down to the back of the club, and with help he put two barrels on each cow— strapping the barrels so that one was on each side of a cow. The animals were then driven to the hut where Jimmy and his friends gathered. There they proceeded to have a drunken orgy over the next few days. This, I should say, would not harm or hurt the cows. These animals are strong and would be able to take the weight of the barrels. After they had done their duty the cows were returned to their grazing grounds. As it happens, the cows probably belonged to a nephew of my own, who was unlikely to know a thing about this escapade.

Brooking No Rivals

Jimmy was friendly with Maureen, with whom he had grown up. They eventually got married—but at earlier stages other young men showed an interest in the lady. This was a very dangerous thing to do—beyond a certain point. If they persisted it usually meant their landing up in hospital! There was one particularly bad case of an ardent swain. He really fancied Maureen and pursued her. Jimmy attacked him and threw him from the top of the Nine Arches (these carry a railway line over a deep gully). The boy climbed back up, was beaten up again and again thrown into the gully. This was too much, and a man intervened. It seems that both he and the injured boy were taken away in an ambulance.

A Penny for the Guy

One was a shocking incident—but the violence was not altogether intentional. There is a custom around Guy Fawkes time of giving a penny to the guy, and one of Jimmy's pals was normally dressed a bit like a scarecrow. Jimmy and his friends decided to put paper up the arms of his long coat and doctor his face, probably with an old hat etc. He evidently looked a proper guy, and he was mistaken for the normal stuffed dummy. Along came a man who offered one pound to be allowed to have a kick at the guy. This was accepted. To their horror the man, thinking he was attacking a fake, kicked the poor guy fully in the face.

Top Dog

There were still three independent gangs in Gibshill, but by now Jimmy's was the senior one and its leadership was disputed by a man called Pat Graham. He challenged Jimmy and managed to get a chain wrapped round his neck. Jimmy retaliated with a knife. He stabbed him in the arm and body, broke his jaw and fractured his skull. Evidently Jimmy went berserk and didn't fully know what he was doing. As the man was being put into an ambulance Jimmy was still hitting him. As he says now, 'It was only by the grace of God that I never killed anybody.'

Wedding with a Difference

There was a wedding of an American sailor to a local girl in Gibshill. Harry, one of Jimmy's gang, probably drunk, invaded the reception and was found jumping on the three-tiered cake. This was naturally resented by four of the groom's naval friends, who threw Harry out. Jimmy, not knowing the circumstances (not, I suppose, that it would have made much difference if he had), went to his friend's help—but the opposition was too strong for normal measures—so Jimmy went for a hatchet and a scythe and fought the five of them on the street. He hit one man with the hatchet, and Jimmy's father came on the scene and got things stopped. The gang were beginning to gather and very wisely the Americans ran for it. The whole wedding reception was stopped.

Almost Killed

Harry and Jimmy were going into Gibshill one day when a local girl complained to them that a man had hit her on the arm with a car door. This man belonged to an older gang from outside the area, and he was with a number of his friends at a party in Gibshill. Jimmy hit him and the matter escalated into a gang fight. In the mêlée Jimmy got his arm badly gashed through an accident with a window. A main artery was badly damaged, and bones broken. He suffered a great loss of blood and collapsed twice on his way to hospital—to which he walked with Maureen. He was kept in hospital overnight and given transfusions. This was still going on in the morning. Maureen took his blood-drenched clothes home. His mother told her that she had washed her hands of Jimmy and hoped that he would die. Jimmy signed himself out of hospital but refused to stop using his injured arm. It burst open time and again, and eventually to put an end to this the hospital put the arm in a 'stooky' (plaster cast)—but Jimmy still went on fighting. With a stooky arm he was even more dangerous. He came on a man attacking two of his gang with an axe and Jimmy clobbered him with his stooky arm. This felled him and the boys then got the axe.

Riot in Dunoon

On another occasion Jimmy with five of his gang, dressed in white with bovver boots, decided to go to Dunoon, and Jimmy invited Maureen to go with them. This was his way of taking her out (which he seldom did), but he didn't tell her of the gang overtone and their real intentions. They began to drink and ran amok in the middle of a Boys Brigade procession. They smashed drums, trumpets and an amusement arcade. They refused to pay fares going off a bus, and five of them hit the bus driver. Harry, no doubt drunk, fell down a cliff and might have been killed, and Jimmy, now shocked at his past callousness, says that he didn't really care about Harry. He was more interested in getting the vodka which he knew Harry had. Jimmy was in court over this incident. By the time the case came up he was in Glenochil, and in sentencing him the judge banned him from the area for life, on pain of imprisonment if he set foot in it again.

The Beginnings of Change

While in Longriggend, Jimmy found himself in the 'cage' for bullying and stealing from the other prisoners. He eventually graduated to Glenochil, which was noted for a particularly tough regime—which did not, however, trouble

Jimmy, who felt that he emerged from such institutions immensely fit and also more astute. At one point about thirty-five from the Gibby were there, and they evidently dominated the place in spite of the strict discipline. A point came when they were split up and Jimmy had a choice: to spend his weekends locked up alone in his cell or go to Christian services and take a correspondence course on the Bible. He chose the latter and indeed gained certificates; but this did not lead him to a knowledge of Christ. There came, however, a critical moment when Jimmy started to speak to God. He said, 'You'll need to help me. I don't know anything.' He feels he got little help from the chaplain. The man did speak with him, but Jimmy felt he was unreal and the words he spoke had little real significance in the chaplain's own life.

Things gradually began to get better. Jimmy got back to normal life. He stopped drinking, started work, and got married to Maureen. Violence lessened but still occurred occasionally—particularly when the idea got around that he was 'finished'. Normally when a gang leader weakens, an up-and-coming young champion wants to defeat him to earn the kudos that goes with such a victory—but Jimmy wasn't 'finished', and he 'sorted out' three of his attackers to prove it. He also attacked a group who were troubling an old gang leader named Jannetts, whom Jimmy held in very great respect. Breakouts, however, were only occasional, but Jimmy did notice that drinking wines and spirits still stirred something aggressive in him.

It was difficult, moreover, to settle down. As he puts it, people pushed their luck and some took things out on Maureen and tried to break their marriage. From the beginning of their friendship there was trouble over religion. Jimmy's family were Orange, Maureen's were Catholic. Jimmy was not worried about Maureen's remaining a Catholic and going to the chapel as often as she liked— although he did despise fellow criminals who called themelves Cathòlics and lived as he did. He accused them of being liars, hypocrites and phoneys. Jimmy knew that his old lifestyle and true religion did not mix. Maureen, however, did not fall into this category. She was never a gangster, although she did get lifted at the time of the Dunoon episode (when she was only fifteen). Jimmy saw that there was always a reserve about her which attracted him. She was different from the lot who hung around the gang.

So the marriage was not approved by either family and none of them came to the wedding, which was in a registry office, although Maureen's folk provided a spread for a reception. Nobody was present except Maureen's father and mother. Jimmy's family all refused the invitation. The food was left.

Maureen's Salvation

Evidently from an early age Maureen had spiritual desires and longings. She had an ability to read and understand situations and conditions of people she met, although she did not know God. She was hungry for the things of God, and came to a point where she asked Him to reveal Himself to her. This happened while she was in the chapel. She felt it was her spirit rather than her mind which made the request, and she got a shock. There came on her an awesome fear and she wondered if she had done a dangerous thing and would die.

At a critical point Struthers Memorial Church were having an outreach in the City Halls in Glasgow. The special speaker was Jean Darnall. Maureen was right at the back and felt she could hardly see Jean but became very conscious of the presence of Christ. She felt she could discern Him clearly, and when the altar call was given she almost ran out. As it happens, Jean began to minister to the other end of the long line of people in which Maureen waited. Eventually Jean reached her and spoke remarkably. God had taken Maureen back over her past and had dealt closely with her. Jean seemed to realize this and spoke most appropriately about her condition and what lay ahead for her.[1] It was quite amazing how, in spite of great numbers to attend to, Jean Darnall seemed able to give careful time to everyone. There was never a feeling of hurry or of anybody being short-changed. Maureen was gloriously saved that night.

Jimmy's Conversion

Jimmy watched Maureen carefully. He saw a very real change, but still had reservations. He did, however, read Nita Edwards' story in *Miracle in the Mirror* when Maureen was not watching him.[2] If she came in suddenly he quickly got rid of the book. He did not want anybody to know of his secret interest in the things of God. There came a night, however, when Nita was speaking at our summer camp in Wiston, and Jimmy unexpectedly decided to come with Maureen. Miss Mary Black took the worship and I think he liked this. From the start he has had an affinity with Mary. He also heard me take some part and Nita preach. He was not converted that night, but he did buy himself a suit to go to church—a mighty change for the tough gang leader! Meantime he watched people closely and said to himself, 'There must be a way in'—but he couldn't find it. One Sunday morning God spoke to him quite clearly: *I am the Way in*. He went into the vestry after the service and found Christ. He was gloriously saved and greatly rejoiced in his changed condition.

Baptism in the Spirit

On a Friday night a few months later he was baptized in the Holy Spirit. He was greatly elated by this experience. He felt filled with new wine and for two hours after the meeting he sat with tongues flowing freely. Jimmy says that God filled him as he did the apostles of old, and words fail him to describe the experience and the change it brought into his life.

How true the words of Christ: 'Ye shall receive power after that the Holy Ghost is come upon you!'

In Jimmy's life there are four other areas which I would like to refer to in this testimony: his healing from rheumatoid arthritis, his healing from a Pott's fracture, a vision of angels, and his deliverance from demon power.

Healing from Rheumatoid Arthritis

Jimmy suffered painfully from rheumatoid arthritis.[3] A few years ago things reached an unbearable point. He found himself in agony with hands almost locked. Here is his story in his own words:

> For two years I was riddled with rheumatoid arthritis. I used to relieve the pain by going for a freezing cold bath at two in the morning, when Maureen and the kids were all sleeping. I'd sit in the cold water for hours. People might think it's daft going into a bath at two o'clock in the morning, but that was the only thing that helped me. I would then go to bed and get up in the morning all stiff and unable to open my hands. We ran a scrap metal business, and I'd often say to Maureen, 'Well, we can't do a lot of work today because I can't move my hands.' I just prayed to God all the time, 'Lord, if it be Your will I'll be healed.'
>
> But it came to a stage when it was so severe, really so severe, that I would sit down and cry with the pain. It was one of these times that I said, 'Come on, Maureen, I'll need to go home. I can't stand this any more.'
>
> She said, 'Jimmy, I'll take you to the doctor,' and I said, 'Well, that's fine, but they can do nothing for me. They've got nothing for me.'*
>
> So Maureen took me and as we drove on I said,

---

* He had of course sought medical help earlier, but by this time realised that no hope of a cure was held out by his doctor.

'Maureen, you're away past the Health Centre.' She said, 'I'm taking you to the best doctor—Jesus Christ.' I said, 'Well, OK then.'

'We'll go and get Mr Black to pray with you.' So Maureen rapped the door and Mrs Black welcomed us into her house...I was black as an ace of spades! She said, 'Mr Black's not in. He's away on holiday—a day's touring with Grace.'

I just thought, 'Oh, no—nothing doing,' and as I sat there Mrs Black and Maureen started speaking. I was sitting there and the pain was getting so severe in my hands that I couldn't even open them. My left hand was completely closed, and my right hand was starting to close too. Mrs Black said, 'I can go and get Mary to pray with you.' I said, 'That would be good—that would be good.'

As soon as Mary walked into the room I just knew the Presence of God was there and I knew that pain was going to go away from me that day.

Mary started praying with me and as soon as she did so the pain was gone, completely gone. That doesn't happen with this disease, and I just sat there and said, 'Oh, thanks, God. Thank You very much. I don't care if I can't open my hands. I don't care as long as that pain's gone.'

But Mary said, 'Open your hands, Jimmy.'

I said, 'Oh, you'll not get them to open.' But they did. I was amazed. I was opening and shutting them, saying, 'This doesn't happen. This doesn't happen to me.' I really thank God for His faithfulness. He is a faithful God.

Some people told me to watch out for backlashes. I thought, 'There will be no backlashes—I'm healed. I know I'm healed.' But it did happen, one day in the following week when Maureen had just gone away in the truck and I was sitting on the stair of the office. Satan says, 'You're not healed, Jimmy,' and I'm sitting there arguing, 'I am.' He said, 'Well, feel the pain in your hands,' and for a moment I thought I felt a pain in my right hand. And I said, 'No, no,' and I closed my eyes and went into prayer.

When I closed my eyes I saw coming before me Christ Himself. His two hands were open and He said, 'Jimmy, look at these hands. These are the hands that healed you: these are the hands that know pain and suffering.' I looked at His hands and I saw the blood pouring from Christ's hands. I saw the lashes on His chest. I saw the Christ that knows pain. I truly was completely healed.

I really do want to thank Him for what He's done for me this year. I praise His Name.

Before Jimmy testified to his healing, Mary told me of the inner side of her experience in praying with him but insisted that I was not to speak of it before he himself spoke. After his public declaration I invited her to share her experience with the church. Here is her account:

I'd like to say a little of what I saw of Christ in the experience that Jimmy has described, because it was very beautiful—the touch of the personality of Christ that came in.

First of all there was an acute sense of the compassion of Christ, and what struck me was how different Christ's compassion is from human compassion. Often human compassion goes out to the sufferer and suffers with that one but does not always have the antidote to heal, and therefore the compassion is tinged with pain and with sadness. But Christ's compassion was living, active and full of joy because it was going to heal. That was a beautiful thing. In this case there was a very steady and joyous touch of the compassion of the Lord Jesus Christ, which was really exquisite.

The second thing that struck me was how easy it is for Christ to heal. It's no bother to Him at all, and it is lovely to think that if there is just enough of the Presence of Christ in a place, healing can occur so easily. Let me make it quite clear: I believe that in this case Christ was determined to heal and that a healing process had already begun the week before [when Jimmy had received prayer for his condition], and that God was minded to carry that through irrespective of the channel. There was a sense that Christ was present in the atmosphere to do it, and when the Presence of Christ is strongly enough there you feel that healing can just flow from His fingers so easily.

The third thing was that as I felt Christ's hands touch Jimmy's hands, I knew them as the nail-pierced hands of Christ—the hands that knew suffering. It was beautiful. The reason I asked Jimmy to turn his hands round and open them after we prayed was because after I'd seen the nail-pierced hands of Christ in my spirit, I felt that I saw Christ turn his hands upwards—I saw the hands of Christ at Calvary turned over and in the moment that His hands turned over I felt as if something fled away—as if something went up from His hands. It was as if Christ was saying, 'The hands are empty of pain,' and somehow I felt it was important to ask Jimmy to turn his hands over as well. I do really bless God for the wonderful experience of Christ that came into that room. I think all of us were just flooded with His Presence. I delight in Jimmy's healing, as no doubt he does too, but I have a feeling that perhaps Jimmy delights even more in just that wonderful sense of the love of God that came down on him—isn't that right, Jimmy? [*Jimmy was present and agreed.*] The loveliness of Christ that flooded down on the four of us was really wonderful. What I really seek is that that Presence of Christ will intensify amongst us and be abundantly there in all our gatherings, and that it will be that which really excites us. Jesus is present to heal. The actual healings are wonderful, but, oh—if I could just introduce you to that Christ, and make you conscious of such a divine compassion and such a light and beauty, I would be thrilled beyond words. How lovely is the action of the divine—praise His glorious Name.

One of our nurses had told me earlier that rheumatoid arthritis just doesn't get better. There are two types of arthritis: rheumatoid and osteoarthritis, and the first of these is extremely serious. She said of Jimmy's case, 'This is an outstanding miracle. It's like the healing of cancer.'

So there was 'no cure'. But God! Blessed be His Name.

Pott's Fracture Healed

One day Jimmy and Maureen arrived unexpectedly at the church bookshop in the days when this was in its old premises. Jimmy was limping very badly. Indeed I have the impression of him almost hopping. Maureen announced that they had come to get his ankle healed, and she seemed to be quite sure this would happen. I was to pray for him. Wonderful, I thought—with a marked lack of faith!

Evidently Jimmy had been trying to break a piece of wood a few days earlier. He had placed this against a wall at an angle and jumped on it. The wood was tougher than he had expected and he was thrown off, twisting his ankle badly. He neglected this and of course found himself in real trouble.

When I saw the state he was in I was very solicitous. I quickly secured a chair for him but since there were a few folks in the shop I felt I could not very well pray for him there. He was in too much pain to be directed downstairs to the church or the vestry. The hall upstairs was in use as a tearoom—so that didn't suit either. I took him into the kitchen, which is quite small, and sat him in a chair in the middle of the floor while I squatted down beside him on a makeshift contraption. Maureen came in too. I placed my hands round the injured ankle and prayed. Now I am not going to claim that I was full of faith; Maureen on the other hand seemed to have no doubt that Jimmy was going to be healed. She felt sure that God had promised this. Indeed as they were leaving their house to come to the church, a neighbour, seeing the state Jimmy was in, asked if they were going to the hospital. 'No,' she said, 'I'm taking him to the church to be healed.' The neighbour was very sceptical about that. 'You wait and see,' said Maureen, 'we'll be coming back at five o'clock and you'll see: he'll be healed.'

Suddenly it was as though there came a bolt from the blue and Jimmy was healed instantly. He bent down and put his shoe on. His foot now went into the shoe without any difficulty. My recollection is that it had been dangling from his toes previously. He got up and left me there sprachling (sprawling) on the floor, my support having collapsed. I picked myself up with some difficulty and followed the pair of them back into the shop. I shall not easily forget reactions from witnesses there.

One of them at first would not, could not believe it. Another, Joyce, had called to me as we had gone into the kitchen, 'If he gets healed—what about my ear?' (She suffers from tinnitus and deafness in one ear.) Now the colour drained out of her face with shock.

Jimmy began to do a little jig up and down the shop. He

put his weight on the ankle with no difficulty at all. Something very real seemed to have happened. We were very pleased but also in a kind of state of shock. Now I don't come out of this very well. I found myself thinking (maybe because I'm an old Scotsman), 'Everybody wants to be healed, and sometimes there is wishful thinking.' I am maybe naturally a bit of a sceptic—a terrible admission for a leader to make—but I thought, 'I'll watch Jimmy when nobody's looking at him and see if the limp comes back. When he leaves for home I'll watch him going along the lane outside.' I had a long time to wait, for he and Maureen started washing the dishes and stayed in the shop for about two hours. There he was dancing up and down, hopping from foot to foot with never a twinge. And I did spy on him as he walked away—totally unaware of being observed. He was as sprightly as a bird. There was never a sign of a limp.

When Jimmy had first arrived at the shop, Mary, an ambulance driver, had been present with her unsaved adult niece. On seeing Jimmy's ankle and learning that it had been injured some days earlier she had claimed, 'You're going to be in trouble. When they get you in hospital they'll go for you for neglecting it for so long. That's a Pott's fracture.'

By the time Jimmy came back into the bookshop healed, Mary and her niece had gone. The niece had been shocked at what she had initially heard, and as they left said to her aunt, 'Do these people really think that that ankle will be healed?' I have the impression that she thought we were all *doolally*—to use a modern expression. When she heard the news of the healing she was evidently profoundly impressed and totally silenced. And so to the final stage. Jimmy and Maureen did get home at the time promised and they saw the sceptical neighbour. It was obvious that Jimmy was healed, and there was never a sign of a hospital visit.

The healing was permanent and there were no after effects.

A Vision of Angels

In addition to his remarkable healings, Jimmy with Maureen was privileged to have very close contact with angels on one memorable occasion. This is described in *Christ the Deliverer*, but the experience was of such interest and significance that I reproduce the account here almost in full. The details were largely supplied by Maureen after one of my proofreaders had objected that an earlier reference to the incident had not been sufficiently explicit. 'People', he wrote, 'will want to know the details right down to the street in which it happened.'[4]

Approximately two and a half years after her salvation, Maureen and Jimmy had just retired to bed at 12:35 on a Wednesday morning. No sooner had they set the alarm clock than Maureen heard a sound as of sweet voices and said to Jimmy, 'Hear them sweet voices?'—a colloquial way of putting things! She thought they were like children's voices—sweet and gentle. She got up and opened the blind and looked out to the garden. There, about twenty-four feet away, she distinctly saw two angels. Commenting on the distance, she said that while there was distance, there was also a sense of there being no distance. One angel was male and the other female.[5] Jimmy had come up behind Maureen when she opened the blinds and the angels were facing them directly. The male angel was standing still but the female angel was lifting and passing her left wing over her face in a constant motion. (This reminded me of Isaiah's description of the cherubim with six wings: 'each one had six wings; with twain he covered his face, and with twain he covered his feet, and with twain he did fly.'*)

Maureen had the impression that the angels were attempting to convey something to them and that the

---

* Isa 6:2.

motion of the wing was significant. She later felt that by their attitude and motion they were indicating that a Greater than themselves was present—that God the Almighty was there. She felt that if they hadn't been in Christ the experience would have killed them. They felt protected by Christ. This part of the experience seemed to take place in a few moments, but in reality an hour had passed. Where it went they have never understood. They had first felt captivated but there came a moment when they had an urgent desire to turn and run—as though instructed to go. This they did and suddenly there was a flash everywhere. Where the light which was not of earth came from, they do not know. It was light but—as Maureen expresses it—it was 'different light'. A quick flash went right through the house.

By this time they had made their way to the living room. They were so shaken that they couldn't stand upright. Maureen in her graphic way described how she put her back to one wall and slithered down it. She looked across and there was Jimmy slithering down the opposite wall. All this time they were both speechless and had said not one word to each other about what had happened.

It seems that in this room a fuller realization came of what the angels had been trying to communicate. 'A knowledge of the Godhead', Maureen says, 'was there. Although things happened so quickly, knowledge was given.' Something she describes as being like a powerful aura came in and 'we seemed to absorb something of it. There was knowledge in it too.' (This reminds me of the words in 1 Corinthians 13: 'Then shall we know even as we are known'—a way of knowing which bypasses the mind. It is something like this that I think Maureen is trying and finding difficult to express.)

Her mind, she felt, just could not cope with what was happening, with what she had seen and known. One part of her would have loved somebody to convince her that it was her imagination, that it wasn't true, that her mind was not affected. This was something beyond her for which she was not mentally prepared. She was disoriented. Her brain, she said, could not take it in. It was trying to refuse acceptance of the event and indeed she wondered if she was going out of her mind. Maureen's heart, however, was at peace. All was well and indeed wonderful at a deeper level. As she puts it, 'There was a knowing there.'

The next part is very typical of the lady concerned, and indeed maybe of ladies more generally! She decided that she would tell Jimmy nothing—not one thing of what she had seen or how she had felt—until he had told her everything of what he had seen and felt!! Just so! 'Tell me everything,' she said. 'I'll do better,' he replied; 'I'll draw it for you'—and she says that he had it exactly: one angel was male and the other female. 'What', she asked, 'did you feel?' 'Power,' he replied, 'power.'

The angels, they recognized, were servants, and even from servants such power came. What must God Himself be like? There seemed to come over the two observers a sense of the awesome power of God. 'So great,' Maureen said, 'it could kill you.' Evidently they knew they could not go back into the room from which they had seen the angels. They were very shaken and slept in the living room. This arrangement continued until the weekend.

On the Wednesday forenoon, Maureen told Joan, one of her leaders, at their weekly meeting about her experience, and this was soon communicated to me. Joan suggested that it should not be too quickly and too generally spoken of. She asked her if she had prayed. This Maureen had been afraid to do but did so then. She indicates that she went into a 'large place', feeling like a small speck under a limitless sky.

In the house the Presence remained. They still could not go into the room of the vision. It felt, Maureen said, as though it was God's sanctuary. He dwelt there. The room, she felt, 'would consume you; you couldn't go there'. This continued until the Sunday night. On that occasion a num-

ber of friends were in for supper in the evening, amongst
them a sister-in-law Anne and her friend Grace from Aber-
deen. Folks left for home, and, again at 12:35 a.m., another
sister-in-law phoned to say that Anne and Grace were
strangely affected. Deeply agitated, they wanted to find a
church. They came back to Maureen's home and were
evidently spiritually starving and seeking God. For about
nine months Maureen had been speaking to Anne about the
things of God with little effect—but this time Anne was
certainly affected, and seemingly by direct supernatural
intervention. The earlier gathering in the house had not
been a meeting—but I fully believe the atmosphere in the
house must have been so potent that it brought conviction
of sin and a hunger for God.[6]

'Get down on your knees,' said Maureen. 'God can do it
Himself.'

God's Presence, she reports, came down like a blanket
over the whole room. She laid hands on the two and led
them, as she puts it, 'in the sinner's prayer'. They were both
saved and baptized in the Spirit then and there. After
salvation one of them had said, 'There's mair, there's mair,'
and indeed there was—there was the glorious baptism of
power.

In that room it is apparently very easy to relax and go
into the Spirit. The Presence lingers still—but, says
Maureen, 'The heaviness of the Presence—that which was
too strong for me to be too close to—has lifted.' Evidently
this happened after the salvation and baptism of Anne and
Grace.

There are some further points of interest.

1) About two nights before the visitation, Jimmy and
Maureen were praying silently in the house and had a sense
as though incense was rising within their beings to God.
Otherwise they had no indication of the coming of the
angels.

2) Again and again this story has had a profound effect
upon hearers, whether told publicly or privately.

3) For those further interested, like Alistair, the address of the street in Port Glasgow in which these things happened is 86 Mackie Avenue. The house is still there and so are Maureen and Jimmy.

4) In speaking to a company about this incident I was asked all manner of questions about the angels, and I suppose their interest will be typical of many readers of this book. When I confessed that I had not questioned Jimmy and Maureen closely on certain points, they looked on me rather pityingly, or perhaps rather the way a teacher looks on a disappointing pupil. I consequently made amends with further detail.

Jimmy and Maureen were questioned again, this time very closely, and they supplied a wealth of information. I proceeded to write this up and felt a strange reserve over certain aspects of it. Shortly afterwards Jimmy and Maureen approached me with a feeling of disquiet. They were afraid that there was a wrong focusing of attention on matters of detail related to the angels, instead of full attention going to God. They feared a mistaken attempt to dissect spiritual things in a natural way. Believing they were right in their feeling, I accordingly omitted some of what I had sketched. I could not but remember that where Christ Himself is concerned the Bible has not emphasized His physical appearance and says nothing about certain things which would have attracted merely human interest. In the case of the angels, some additional material may be included.

The angels appeared as angels and not in human guise. Faces were without blemish—indeed there was a sense of perfection of appearance.

One very interesting question to emerge was the source of light. The night was very dark and the window of the bedroom opened to a garden and beyond it to a hillside. There was neither moonlight nor starlight nor any source of artificial light. The question did not occur to Maureen, since on opening the blinds she saw the angels clearly.

Jimmy, however, before going to the window, became aware of light coming into the room and wondered where it came from. The only feasible explanation is that the light came from the angels themselves. Later, of course, there came the more intense flash of light which seems to have been entirely supernatural—as earlier indicated, a light that did not rise on earth.

Jimmy and Maureen emphasized that 'what the angels were giving off, you were drinking in'. There appears to have been a spiritual emanation from the heavenly beings to the humans. Life was transmitted and absorbed. Maureen and Jimmy felt like two small specks in a vast *spiritual dimension*.

At nine o'clock in the morning Jimmy went out to examine the garden. He wanted to see if any marks had been left on the ground. He even looked in the hut and all around it—but there were no evidences of the visitation. Maureen had evidently told him (or asked—I'm not sure which!) to go out at 4:30—but, as he explained, he felt braver at nine!

Deliverance

It is time to stand back and have an objective look at Jimmy Lunan's life. Wonderful, you might exclaim. There he is, saved from a life of real violence, truly converted, baptized in the Holy Spirit, twice miraculously healed and granted a vision of angels. Surely this man is 'home and dry'! In addition to all this, his life was giving evidence of a very deep change. In the days of his violence, apart from Maureen he had known little love. He neither gave it or received it. His position as gang leader was held through fear. There was neither love nor respect. His had been a hard, cruel life, and he had been a hard, cruel and very lonely man. Now he was surrounded by love—he knew himself to be loved and cared for, but perhaps more significantly he knew what it was to love. He had changed to a caring, gentle person. I have come to regard him as one of nature's gentlemen, always courteous and considerate. Was this not all that could reasonably be expected? Indeed, no.

Long ago I learned that while God could save a soul in an instant of time, even when there had been a lifetime of deep bondage to Satan, that did not mean that all bondage was immediately broken. There is a difference between salvation from the penalty and salvation from the power of sin. I had come to recognize that just as a person may be saved and still have a disease such as cancer, so he or she may know true salvation and have one part of their spiritual being affected by demon power and in need of deliverance. Since I have written about this extensively in other books[7] I will not expand on it here, but come back to Jimmy's case.

For a long time we had no urge to raise the subject with Jimmy. At first he had avoided services at which I was preaching. He did not like to be too deeply probed. But even after that phase had passed there was no liberty to emphasize his need for deliverance. Then came a change.

I think Jimmy himself gradually became aware that there was something deep down that needed sorted. Maureen had known very real deliverance and he knew this. A time came when she very clearly knew of his need and indeed prayed with him about it. Significantly Mrs Grace Gault, one of our leaders who is used in the ministry of deliverance, became burdened about Jimmy, and very soon afterwards Jimmy approached her. I knew what was afoot and watched them depart for the vestry at the end of a service. Sure enough, Grace quite soon appeared at the vestry door and gave me a signal. I knew that there could be a real danger of violence if Jimmy was to be set free, and I gathered a group of strong helpers to go into the vestry. I had not thought that Jimmy would be intentionally violent, but I knew that if demons of deep violence surfaced Jimmy might be very difficult to control, and might have to be saved from what they would try to do through him. In other words, he might have to be physically restrained during the actual deliverance.

This proved to be the case. Jimmy was a gentleman and wanted to hurt nobody—but he was himself very aware of the danger to others as evil powers might become manifest through him. As the critical point came, there was violent disturbance while Jimmy was physically controlled, but God triumphed and the demons were compelled to leave his body. It was a glorious victory.

He said a very interesting thing when he came back to a normal state: 'You know, I could see what the demon was doing. It was looking round to see if there was anybody in that group uncovered, whom it could attack or enter. People could have been in real danger from it. Fortunately everybody was covered, not all equally deeply, but all covered.'

I have questioned Jimmy about this, and it seems that there were those of us who were deeply covered by God as by an invisible shield, and in a position to deal with demons aggressively and successfully. Others perhaps because of the circumstances of the occasion had covering enough for their personal safety—but could otherwise have been in real danger, especially if they had attempted deliverance on their own. This is a point worth pondering and remembering in a day when it has become fashionable for many to involve themselves in this ministry who have never been really called of God into it. It is a dimension in which we should move very carefully indeed—in fact one in which we should not move at all, but only be moved of God.[8]

A Truly Remarkable Story

As was said in summing up Allan's testimony, surely this too is a truly remarkable story by any standard, and again the glory is all God's. Here we see a man changed from a depraved condition to a veritable son of God, from deep sin to holiness—and the road for Jimmy has not been easy. He gave up the business he was in for moral reasons (there was so much corruption around it) and accepted a measure of deprivation as a result. He held to his principles through tough times and now, even in the material sphere, things are working out for him.

Maureen was also baptized in the Spirit and at a later point she too experienced wonderful deliverance as described elsewhere. Their marriage, in spite of its beginnings, has been a very good one. They have always cared for each other and stayed together through thick and thin. They have not been without problems, but overall there is so much for which God has the glory.

Up from the pit to the heavenlies: from gangland to Glory Land indeed! Praised be His Name.

Here lies the justification for the title of our new edition of *Reflections on the Baptism in the Holy Spirit*, now renamed *The Baptism in the Spirit and Its Effects*. Surely the baptism is a mighty experience and its effects are beyond our understanding. To have lives changed as Allan's and Jimmy's have been changed is miraculous—but, thank God, our God is a miracle-working God.

Notes

[1] Maureen says that when Jean reached her she said words like these: 'You know Him, don't you?' Maureen assented—for she had truly been meeting Christ. Jean continued, 'You have been hurt so deeply and badly, but Christ has come to take it away.' Maureen had in fact suffered intensely all her life from an ability to see into the spiritual realm without having the protective shield of Christ. She was aware of demonic activity sometimes concentrated in particular areas (though she had never heard of 'territorial spirits'. She would sometimes urge Jimmy to come away from a particular environment because of its 'influence') and sometimes affecting herself. She was terrified and defenceless; she felt she could turn to nobody, for fear of being thought crazy. Darkness seemed very close at hand, and God very remote. She concluded that death was the key to seeing God clearly. Now with Jean's words to her she discovered that she need not wait till death to be delivered from her predicament. The full story of her deliverance, when there came a mental flashback to the night in the City Hall, is told in my

forthcoming book on spiritual warfare (New Dawn Books, 1995). For a briefer account see my *Christ the Deliverer* (New Dawn Books, 1991), p. 78.

2 Nita Edwards and Mark Buntain with Ron Hembree and Doug Brendel, *Miracle in the Mirror* (Torbay Publishing, 1982).

3 This account is taken from *Christ the Deliverer*, pp. 79–82.

4 *Christ the Deliverer*, p. 105. The account which follows is adapted from pp. 105–11. As I indicate *ibid.*, p. 78, having had experiences myself with angels I had no difficulty in accepting this account completely. Scripture has many examples of angelic visitations and of conversations between angels and men. In revival it frequently happens. On one occasion in Lewis, one old man evidently remarked to a friend, 'Revival will break out over there tonight'— naming a village. 'How do you know it will break out there?' 'Oh, I saw the angels going over this afternoon.'

5 Some readers may feel surprise at the idea of one angel being male and the other female—perhaps because of Christ's saying that 'in the resurrection they neither marry, nor are given in marriage, but are as angels in heaven' (Mat 22:30). But note, this does not say that angels are without gender, but merely that they do not marry. Masculinity and femininity are not expected to be changed in us in that state—so there seems no reason to assume that there is no such differentiation amongst angels. The comparison of our state with that of the angels may even imply the contrary.

6 This, I trust, is a portent of revival. When that comes, people are converted in their homes, on the streets, at their work. The atmosphere is such that people become God-conscious and break before Him. Preaching is used but often God Himself acts in other ways. He seemed to do so in this case.

7 The subject of deliverance is treated in various of my books: *Reflections on the Gifts of the Spirit*, *Christ the Deliverer*, *Reflections from David*, *Christian Fundamentals*, *Revival: Living in the Realities*, and a forthcoming volume on spiritual warfare (all published by New Dawn Books).

8 I remember speaking to a woman greatly used of God outwith our circles altogether, working with the oppressed and the child-abused, working deeply against Satan. She told me that when she comes against some of the people deeply involved in the occult, immediately the possessing demons look to see if there is a point of weakness in her which might be exploited. It is dangerous to be involved in this kind of work without the covering of God, without the call of God, without holiness.

APPENDIX I

Modern Instances of Tongues being Understood

From *Pentecostal Rays* by George Jeffreys[1]

MARATHI WOMAN SPEAKS IN ENGLISH

A gracious Pentecostal revival came to Mukti, the home where Pandita Ramabai had gathered some two thousand widows and orphans under her care. In the early part of 1907, Albert Norton, that venerable missionary of Dhond, wrote: 'About six months ago we began to hear of Christian believers in different places and countries receiving the gift of speaking in a new tongue, which they had never known before. Our hearts were stirred by these accounts, some of them having come from those whom we have known for years as most humble, earnest, and devoted servants of the Lord. One week ago to-day, I visited the Mukti mission at Kedgaon, thirteen miles from here.

Miss Abrams asked me if I would not like to go into a room where about twenty girls were praying. After entering, I knelt by a table on one side, with closed eyes. Presently I heard someone near me praying very distinctly in English. I was struck with astonishment, as I knew that there was no-one in the room who could speak English, besides Miss Adams. I opened my eyes, and within three feet of me, on her knees, with closed eyes and raised hands, was a woman, whom I had baptized at Kedgaon in 1899, nearly eight years ago, and whom my wife and I had known intimately since as a devoted Christian worker. Her mother tongue was Marathi, and she could speak a little Hindustani. But she was utterly unable to speak or understand English, such as she was using. But when I heard her speak English idiomatically, distinctly, and fluently, I was as impressed as I would have been had I seen one, whom I knew to be dead, raised to life. A few other illiterate Marathi women and girls were speaking in English, and some were speaking in other languages which none of us at Kedgaon understood. This was not gibberish, but it closely resembled the speaking of foreign languages to which I have listened, but did not understand.

Again I was at Mukti last Saturday and Lord's Day, where some twenty-four persons had received the gift of tongues. Quite a number had received the ability to speak in English, a language before unknown to them. Just why God enabled these women and girls to speak in English, instead of Tamil, Bengali, Tugulu, or some other language of India, unknown to them, I cannot say. But I have an idea that it is in mercy to us poor missionaries from Europe and America, who as a class, seem to be doubting Thomases in regard to the gifts and workings of the Spirit, and are not receiving the power of the Holy Ghost as we ought, and we shall wish that we had done, when we are entered into the world to come.

TONGUES USED TO CONVERT JEWISH DOCTOR

Another instance of a Hebrew being saved through the ministry of speaking in tongues is that of Dr Florence Murcutt, now of Manhattan Beach, California, who is an Australian Jewess and was brought up in the Jewish faith. She was taught by her mother that she must never believe that Jesus was the Son of God. Having an enquiring mind, on the death of her mother she read through the whole Word of God from cover to cover in six weeks. After having secured her medical degree in the city of Philadelphia, she first came in contact with the Pentecostal people in Vancouver, British Columbia. She was travelling down from Vancouver to Los Angeles, and stopped off at Portland, Oregon, where there was a Pentecostal camp meeting. She saw the signs following, and there were many saved and healed and filled with the Spirit at the meeting. One night she stood close by the tent where there were ten Canadians standing. She was conversing with them when one Canadian brother, who was under the anointing of God, began to speak to her, addressing her in the purest Parisian French, a language with which she was familiar. Dr Murcutt says: 'He told me I was a sinner, and that I could only be saved in one way, and that was through Jesus Christ who was the Way, the Truth and the Life. He told me that Jesus was the Door, and that I would have to enter by that door. He told me that He was the Bread of Life, and that I would have to be sustained by Him. As he spoke he urged me to yield to God. This brother was absolutely unfamiliar with Parisian French, but was speaking entirely under the anointing of God. He told me that this Pentecostal outpouring was of God, and that it was the Latter Rain which God had promised to send in the last days. The Spirit through him gave a full revelation of the truth concerning the Trinity. We talked for over an hour in Parisian French. When I said anything that tallied with the Word of God, the Spirit of God in this brother rejoiced. When I said anything contrary to the Word of God, the Spirit of God in him would moan. As a result of this manifestation of God's presence, I went on my knees and yielded to God.' For many years Dr Murcutt has been serving the Lord, and has been greatly blessed as an evangelist among both English-speaking people and Latin Americans.

Note

[1] pp. 157–160.